WULFRUN
COLLEGE

D0277527

Children excluded from primary school

Children excluded from primary school

Debates, evidence, responses

Carol Hayden

Open University Press
Buckingham • Philadelphia

Open University Press
Celtic Court
22 Ballmoor
Buckingham
MK18 1XW

and

1900 Frost Road, Suite 101
Bristol, PA 19007, USA

First Published 1997

A catalogue record of this book is available from the British Library

ISBN   0 335 19562 8 (pbk)   0 335 19563 6 (hbk)

Library of Congress Cataloging-in-Publication Data
Hayden, Carol, 1955–
    Children excluded from primary school : debates, evidence,
responses / Carol Hayden.
        p.   cm.
    Includes bibliographical references and index.
    ISBN 0–335–19563–6 (hbk).   ISBN 0–335–19562–8 (pbk)
    1. Student expulsion—Great Britain.   2. Problem children—
Education—Great Britain.   I. Title.
LB3089.4.G7H39   1997
371.5′43′0941—dc20
                                                              96–24013
                                                              CIP

Typeset by Graphicraft Typesetters Limited, Hong Kong
Printed in Great Britain by St Edmundsbury Press,
Bury St Edmunds, Suffolk

Contents

Abbreviations

ACE	Advisory Centre for Education
ADD	attention deficit disorder
ADHD	attention deficit/hyperactivity disorder
AEP	Association of Educational Psychologists
AMA	Association of Metropolitan Authorities
CRE	Commission for Racial Equality
CTC	city technology college
DfE	Department for Education (formerly DES, Department of Education and Science, now DfEE, Department for Education and Employment)
DoH	Department of Health
EBD	emotional and behavioural difficulties
EOTAS	education other than at school
EP	educational psychologist
ERA	Education Reform Act (1988)
ESN	educationally sub-normal
EWO	education welfare officer
FA	formal assessment (for special educational needs)
FAS	Funding Agency for Schools
GCSE	General Certificate of Secondary Education
GEST	Grants for Education Support and Training
GMS	grant maintained school
HMI	Her Majesty's Inspectorate
ILEA	Inner London Education Authority
INSET	in-service training
LEA	local education authority

LMS	local management of schools
MLD	moderate learning difficulties
NAHT	National Association of Head Teachers
NAS/UWT	National Association of Schoolmasters/Union of Women Teachers
NCE	National Commission on Education
NERS	national exclusions reporting system
NSPCC	National Society for the Prevention of Cruelty to Children
NTA	Non-teaching assistant
NUT	National Union of Teachers
OECD	Organization for Economic Cooperation and Development
OFSTED	Office for Standards in Education
PRU	pupil referral unit
QTA	qualified teaching assistant
SEN	special educational need
SHA	Secondary Heads Association
SNA	special needs assistant
SSD	social services department
SSI	social services inspectorate
TES	*Times Educational Supplement*
VA	voluntary aided (schools)
VC	voluntary controlled (schools)
WO	Welsh Office

Preface

He was rejected from two schools . . . He felt nobody wanted him or liked him . . . He was here all day. He wouldn't dress, he wouldn't wash, he wouldn't eat. He was just like sitting on the chair watching the telly all the time.

> (comment made by the mother of a 7-year-old boy permanently excluded from two schools)

Chris was the first child I'd had to do it with [i.e. permanently exclude him from school]. I agonized for a whole day before I did it . . . I knew, knowing all of the situation Chris was in, that I was doing exactly the same as everybody else had done to him in school and elsewhere. We wanted him to be happy at school and be with all of us. I felt let down by the support I was getting . . . It shouldn't have happened. The poor little devil had been doing so well. I feel so badly . . . but what alternatives did I have?

> (comment made by the head teacher of the same child)

These comments give some insight into the complex circumstances and possible impact on the child of permanent exclusion from primary school. Exclusion from school, or being sent home from school temporarily or permanently, is not a new phenomenon, although evidence suggests that officially recorded permanent exclusion from school of primary age children was almost unheard of until the 1990s.

Only head teachers, or their deputies acting for them in their absence, can exclude a child from school. The right of head teachers to exclude a pupil from school (then referred to as suspension) is enshrined in the 1944 Education Act, which describes the procedure and power to exclude in the following way: 'the power of suspending pupils from attendance for any cause which [the head teacher] considers adequate, but on suspending any pupil [the head teacher] shall forthwith report the case to the governors who shall consult the Local Education Authority' (quoted in Lowenstein 1990: 35). The vagueness of this power meant that it was possible for schools to abuse it. The Education (No. 2) Act 1986 was an attempt to address the issues of proper procedure and common justice in the suspension and expulsion processes (Lovey *et al.* 1993).

'Exclusion' is a relatively new term utilized in relation to children out of school. Most adults will be more familiar with the terms 'suspension' or 'expulsion', which are much more accurate terms than exclusion (*Education* 1993a). Exclusion is a term which has become more common relatively recently and particularly since the 1986 Education Act (ACE 1991). Until September 1994 there were three types of official exclusion which were categorized as: fixed term (less than five days), indefinite, and permanent. The Education Act 1993 abolished indefinite exclusions with effect from September 1994 because it was believed that the very imprecision of the term 'indefinite' left this type of exclusion open to abuse (Gibson 1994). There is another type of exclusion which is outside the focus of the research reported upon in this book, that is the 'unofficial exclusion'. Unofficial exclusions are the 'arrangements' or 'agreements' between parent or carer and schools, which in effect mean that a child has time out of school for a 'cooling off' period or sometimes agrees to leave a school altogether. Stirling (1991) has found such exclusions to be more numerous than officially recorded ones.

Although the Education Act 1993 has added some refinements and changes to procedure with regard to exclusion and has removed the 'indefinite' category, the existence of exclusion as a sanction is not called into question. Head teachers still have the power to exclude and must be supported by the governing body of their school. Local education authorities (LEAs) can overturn decisions in LEA schools only. Time limits have been introduced into the management of permanent exclusion. The 1993 Act places a duty on LEAs to provide education other than at school (EOTAS) and the money follows the excluded pupil (DfE 1994b). Schools can legally exclude a child for up to three fixed term periods a term, that is a total of 15 days a term or 45 days in a school year (DfE 1994b). Exclusion from school is thus firmly sanctioned in law, as is the part-time education of children outside schools.

The research reported upon in this book is concerned with exploring both the home and school circumstances which surround the exclusion of young children from school, as well as broader considerations about how exclusion from school may be related to education policy. It includes investigations into less serious school exclusions which last a matter of days (fixed term) as well as the more serious types of exclusion, known as indefinite (now abolished) and permanent. Primary school children have rarely been the main focus of most exclusions research, yet they number about one in eight of all permanent exclusions. The young age of primary school children may make them more vulnerable when they are out of school, in a number of ways, in comparison with their adolescent counterparts excluded from secondary schools. More optimistically, there may be greater possibilities for the prevention of more entrenched problems, as well as the successful reintegration into mainstream schooling, with more focused and appropriate support for this smaller group of excluded children.

The research which informs this book took place over a two-year period (September 1993 to August 1995) and was funded by the ESRC (Economic and Social Research Council), at the SSRIU (Social Services Research and Information Unit) at the University of Portsmouth. Carol Hayden was the main researcher for the project and was responsible for the research design. Derek Ward (Chapter 5, with Carol Hayden) was a research assistant to the project. Derek is now working with families as a community psychiatric nurse. Christine Sheppard also works at the SSRIU as a research fellow and has conducted her own research into the provision for children with behaviour problems.

The book is divided into three main sections. Section 1 will consider the debates about why exclusion from school is happening and will summarize the findings from previous research. Section 2 will present evidence from the research project, which will include data at national and local authority level, but will concentrate on case studies of excluded children. Case studies will be presented from the points of view of parents and carers, some of the children themselves, as well as teachers. Section 3 will consider institutional responses to exclusion and point towards what is being done and what needs to be done to halt and ultimately reduce the increase in records of primary school exclusion.

Section 1

The debates

One

The context: markets, institutions, families and individuals

Background

A central concern in the development of education policy during the 1980s, leading up to the Education Reform Act 1988 and since, has been about academic standards. This is a concern which has a long history and has been a recurrent feature of debates within and between the main political parties and has come to the fore at various periods in British history (Green 1987). It was the speech of a Labour prime minister, James Callaghan, at Ruskin College Oxford in 1976, which is credited with launching what has come to be known as the 'Great Debate' on education. Control over education and education expenditure may be viewed as a battleground between central and local government since 1979. Education forms the largest area of expenditure for local authorities and the joint second largest area of expenditure (with the health service) for central government. The volume of education legislation passed from 1980 onwards has become legendary as has the beleaguered and ever changing face of the Secretary of State for Education. Undoubtedly the rapid changes brought about in schools by this legislation have created enormous upheavals and stress in schools. Schools in common with other parts of the public sector now operate in a form of market, with the attendant competition for 'customers' between schools in some areas, as well as the concern for the management of image and thus 'marketability' and the income which may follow successful marketing. Competition between schools and accountability through performance indicators have been a major part of the educational reforms which have attempted to address concern about academic standards (McVicar 1991).

Quasi-markets in education

Although many writers loosely refer to a 'market system' in education, the system may be more accurately referred to as a 'quasi-market'. The current organization of the education system might be viewed as a market system inasmuch as individual competitive organizations (providers, i.e. schools) have replaced monopolistic state organizations (i.e. LEAs) as providers. It may be more specifically viewed as a quasi-market system because the public sector differs from conventional markets in a number of important ways; for example, quasi-markets do not operate for profit and services are free at the point of delivery (Le Grand and Bartlett 1993).

Quasi-markets were introduced into the education system in England and Wales by the Education Reform Act 1988, although legislation passed earlier in the 1980s had set the scene for many of the changes implemented in 1988. The themes which run through education policy throughout the 1980s can also be identified in other policies at the time: themes such as the desire to reduce public expenditure; the wish to reduce the power of local government; the promotion of 'choice' through a consumerist view of public services; a strengthening of management and a reduction in the power of professionals and unions; the strengthening in the power of intermediate bodies (governing bodies in the case of schools) to curb the power of professionals and local authorities. However, as McVicar (1991: 137) observes, the earlier Acts were to 'pale into insignificance' in comparison with the 1988 Act. The Education Reform Act 1988 (ERA) is credited literally with introducing a new 'ERA' into the education system.

The Education Reform Act 1988 introduced the National Curriculum, linked with attainment targets and testing, which not only created a tremendous upheaval and workload in schools, but also enhanced central government control over schools in terms of curriculum content and made possible the comparison of results between schools. The publication of examination results from secondary schools has led to the notion of 'league tables' of schools, in which schools can be judged by results over other criteria. The Act reinforced the notion of parental 'choice' and thus emphasized the threat of market forces to the less popular, usually less successful, schools. The power of LEAs was further weakened, with increased delegation of budgets from LEAs to schools. From April 1990 onwards, heads and governing bodies of all schools with more than 200 pupils were responsible for all expenditure except capital and certain collective services. The Inner London Education Authority (ILEA) was also abolished at the same time, which may be viewed as a clear indication of just how subordinate local authorities had become to central government (McVicar 1991).

The Education Act 1993 has been described as 'the biggest piece of educational legislation ever enacted in this country' (Rogers 1993: 3). It substantially rewrites parts of the Education Act 1981 concerning children with special educational needs and builds on sections of the 1988 Act in relation to the National Curriculum and grant maintained schools, as well as extending provisions for school inspection. Rogers (1993) views a desire to increase the grant maintained sector of schooling (schools financed directly by central government) as at the heart of this Act.

The overall effect of the changes in the education service has been to create what has been termed a new value context, an argument which could be extended to other public sector services. Ball (1993: 108) describes the situation in the following way:

> The introduction of market forces into the relations between schools means that teachers are now working within a new value context in which image and impression management are more important than the educational process, elements of control have been shifted from the producer (teachers) to the consumers (parents) via open enrolments, parental choice and per-capita funding. In relations with parents, the use of performance indicators and tests places the achievements of students and the work of teachers in a new light.

Competition in the education market is driven by the amount of money each pupil attracted to the school brings. The onus is now on schools to be attractive to parents and thus maximize their income.

Part of this new value context relates to the notion that parents, as consumers of education on behalf of their children, are encouraged to have the power of 'choice' in relation to where their child attends a particular school. By exercising 'choice' parents can in effect move funds around the system· in theory it should give parents the power to let professionals know what they want and do not want for their children. Schools can no longer predict the number of children they will be educating via a head count of the last year in nearby primary schools or population figures for their 'catchment areas'. Catchment areas have in effect been abolished. However, the notion of 'choice', while a real threat to the budget of schools, does not always amount to much of a choice for some parents and in some areas. Furthermore choice is also a misleading concept in relation to what is legally offered, namely the right to express a 'preference'.

Le Grand and Bartlett (1993: 13) caution that the majority of the changes being brought about by quasi-markets in the public sector are very recent and therefore it is not really feasible to assess their empirical consequences for several years. What much of their work and that of their colleagues does is to undertake a theoretical analysis that specifies the conditions under which quasi-markets would meet particular objectives. One such analysis is given by Levačić (1994) who has focused upon four key criteria in relation to the education system: value for money, improvements in educational standards, greater responsiveness to consumer preferences, and equity. These criteria will briefly be considered in turn.

Quasi-markets are likely to provide an efficient use of economic resources in the education system; they encourage cost consciousness and thus attempt to utilize resources (staff and funding) in the most economically efficient ways. Yet such a system undoubtedly conflicts with more human considerations, such as staff morale, workload, commitment and enjoyment of the work and thus, most importantly, the quality of the learning environment for children.

There is potential for conflict between the changes brought about by a focus on value for money and the drive to raise educational standards, although the evidence here is inconclusive. It is perhaps too early to assess fully whether improvements in educational standards are occurring, although in terms of some measurable outcomes it is clear that GCSE exam results, for example, have improved throughout the period of Conservative reform, from the early 1980s onwards (DfE 1995). Yet at the same time there is continued concern expressed about basic standards of literacy and numeracy, a concern which is largely unfounded according to the National Commission on Education (NCE 1995).

Although schools are obviously making more effort to 'market' themselves to future parents as 'customers', Levačić notes that one of the peculiar features of the education market is the reluctance of schools to expand once they have reached full capacity. This is partly because of government restrictions on the expansion of places in popular schools when there are surplus places available in nearby schools. Also, Bartlett (1992) shows that most schools have a limited capacity to expand. There are often real constraints in terms of space and amenity if popular schools do expand to any great extent. There is also a reluctance to create larger school communities. Furthermore there is little evidence of any increase in the range of types of education available, indeed the content of education is prescribed by central government via the National Curriculum. Thus any difference between types of school is largely based on organization and resourcing rather than educational philosophy, method or content.

There is already evidence of concern that quasi-markets in education are unlikely to operate equitably, for a number of reasons. A major issue is that parents are differentially placed within the education market. Some schools are also in a position to select children, and certainly the most popular schools will never have enough places available for all who choose them (Bartlett 1992). An OECD (1994) report says that parents' choice of school is too often determined by race and class divisions. In Britain, in particular, there is a clear hierarchy of schools, further delineated by the publication of league tables of results. Class divisions in Britain are reported to be bound up with parental choice to an extent which does not exist in the other five countries studied in the OECD report.

For parents to have an effective 'choice' of school the popular and oversubscribed schools need to be able and willing to expand, without damaging the very service which has made them popular. There is then a conflict between this parental choice and a rational use of resources, in a context in which there is a drive to reduce surplus school places. Certain parents and hence their children are likely to benefit more from this apparent choice than others. Edwards and Whitty (1992) have pointed out that the exercise of choice by some parents is likely to diminish the choice of others. If for example there is a decline in the number of parents opting for a particular school, the diminished size and thus budget of that school will reduce the opportunities for the remaining children. This process is also likely to reduce the voices of parents able to make an input into effective change in the school.

Quasi-markets and school exclusion

What has thus been described is a social policy context and the resulting changes within the education service, in which the imperatives for change are not driven primarily by broader educational motives or by the needs of all children. It has been argued that the changes are driven by a desire to reorganize the system in a way which creates pressure to increase measurable academic outputs. It is a policy context which conflicts with other policies, such as increasing integration of children with special educational needs (SEN) and the reduction in residential care and 'out-of-county' placements. Such children are likely to make major demands upon schools which may be difficult to resource appropriately, partly because of the complex nature of the needs some children have. Most notably quasi-markets in education can conflict with the cooperation between services promoted by the Children Act 1989, in relation to children 'in need'. Children in need have not been the focus of the main thrust behind education reforms since 1988, although the Code of Practice (with respect to special educational needs) which came into effect in September 1994 may eventually help to redress the balance (DfE 1994b). One of the clearest criticisms of the effects of a quasi-market in education is the evidence that it does not promote an equitable access to, and distribution of, resources.

In a competitive system somebody loses out, some individuals are in a better position to take part in the competition than others. It has been observed that markets derive their efficiency from the fact that there are 'winners and losers, risk takers and bankruptcies, entrepreneurs and uncertainty' (Veljanovski 1990: 6). Schools have been put under pressure to achieve better examination results, or with younger children, improvements in their attainments in the National Curriculum levels. If they are successful they are the winners who may be rewarded by increased popularity and increasing school rolls. Such schools are better able to plan financially for the future than the less popular schools (the losers), which in a sense risk 'bankruptcy' if they do not improve results sufficiently and compete successfully for children. This competition is occurring at a time when schools are expected to integrate children with a wide range of special educational needs, ranging from physical disability, specific learning difficulties, moderate learning difficulties, sensory impairment, to emotional and behavioural difficulties. Some of these children will make major demands on the resources of a school and particular groups of children may be viewed as more 'deserving' of these resources than others. Yet it has long been stressed by teaching unions that the biggest single impediment to increased academic achievement in schools is the behaviour of a disruptive minority of children. Some of the children with particular types of SEN or disrupted family backgrounds are likely to be (very?) disruptive in school.

Thus the introduction of published league tables of examination results and other indicators of performance in schools has created a climate less likely to be sympathetic to children not only producing no positive contribution to these indicators, but who may also prevent others from doing so. It was predicted by commentators throughout the 1980s (such as DCS 1981, 1991) that the proposed reforms in the Education Reform Act 1988 were likely to marginalize further the most disadvantaged children. Exclusions may be seen as part of the formal representation of this process of marginalization. Stirling (1991) started research in 1989 on the effect of the 1988 Act upon children with emotional and behavioural difficulties. In doing so Stirling was, like Peagram (1991), identifying the specific group of children they expected to be most vulnerable to the changes in the education system. With the benefit of hindsight and growing evidence about the increase in the number of exclusions and with a particular emphasis upon the exclusion of Black pupils, Bourne *et al.* (1994: 10) comment:

> It was inevitable that the Tory reforms would lead to an increase in pupil exclusions from school. Nor could it be expected that a government, which declared its indifference to the potential effects of 'open enrolment' in promoting racial segregation in schools, would give the least consideration to the likely impact of its policies at the other end of the process, in schools' practices of rejecting children through exclusions.

The evidence available to date would suggest that this may indeed be a fair comment upon an initial effect of the introduction of quasi-markets into the education service. However, the long-term effects may be different. Blyth and Milner (1996) speculate upon the possibilities offered by pupils having in effect a potential spending power of approximately £2000 a head at secondary school level. They point to the alternative programmes which are already developing to cater for pupils not attending school, for various reasons, including exclusion. Blyth and Milner go so far as to suggest that it could even be in the interests of some children to be excluded from school, so that they can gain entrance to alternative (and perhaps more appropriate) forms of preferred education. This analysis may be of more relevance to teenagers, most of whom have already spent a decade with their peers in mainstream education; however, the prospects may be less optimistic for young children who have spent only a few years (or less) in school. The potential for long-term social segregation and isolation for young children excluded from school is especially worrying.

Undoubtedly quasi-markets have created great pressures on schools, but whether this aspect of social policy is an adequate explanation for the complex set of circumstances and decisions which surround an exclusion, particularly a permanent exclusion, requires further debate. A number of additional levels of explanation might be considered when interpreting the recorded rise in exclusion. A first consideration must be a careful analysis of the statistics and other information available about the recorded rise in exclusion. It may be that the apparent rise is partly explained by better systems of recording the event in recent years. Although officially recorded exclusions are rising they are relatively speaking still a tiny proportion of all schoolchildren. Copeland (1994: 14) uses the government figures from the NERS exercise to show that permanent exclusion accounts for a fraction of 1 per cent of all pupils. Copeland queries the way the issue has been presented by the media as 'misleading and sensational'. He argues that these figures hardly imply the 'rising tide' referred to in at least one TES front page article (for example, Pyke 1993). Other levels of explanation of exclusion will be briefly considered in the following subsections.

Institution-based explanations of exclusion

Institution-based explanations of children's behaviour leading to exclusion rest upon the belief that any understanding of 'problem' behaviour must depend upon an examination of the way the subject interacts with their environment. It is allied to the interactionist perspective in the sociology of education and has been heavily influenced by a number of key studies, such as that of Cicourel and Kitsuse (1963), Labov (1973) and Hargreaves *et al.* (1975) Interactionists stress the individual skills and attitudes of teachers in explaining why a particular behaviour of a child is viewed as a problem. Other studies, most notably Rutter *et al.* (1979) have emphasized the school effect, in particular school 'ethos' as a major variable in how a particular child or behaviour is viewed. Yet, as Peagram (1993) observes in the 1990s, societal pressures are increasingly directive about what constitutes a problem. There was, for example, a brief consideration by the DfE as to whether they should produce a list of excludable offences, after the publication of the NERS and the passing of the Education Act 1993 (Ward 1994).

The growth of institution-based explanations came after a period in which socio-economic circumstances had been the main focus in much educational research, although psychologists and psychiatrists provided more individualistic explanations. Conventional wisdom, reinforced by most educational research during the 1960s and early 1970s, had argued that academic progress, disruption and attendance are largely determined by pupil background. Research in the late 1970s and during the 1980s (Reynolds *et al.* 1976; Rutter *et al.* 1979; Galloway *et al.* 1982) began to indicate more optimistically that schools themselves make a difference. Some research specifically demonstrated the importance of school organization and ethos in relation to how minor matters could escalate into suspension-worthy offences (Galloway *et al.* 1982; Lawrence *et al.* 1984). McLean (1987) and McManus (1987) showed similar findings in their work. Thus exclusion was viewed as not an inevitable consequence to a particular set of events, but as a product of a set of events dealt with in a particular way. Such research is extremely important in informing the development of systems in schools which are based on notions of natural justice, but by highlighting the role of schools, it also tends to give insufficient consideration to individual and family factors as well as the very real pressures created by education policy. Yet schools are not all responding the same way to the pressures of operating in a quasi-market. If schools were only willing to work with the successes and those who are more amenable, many, many more children would be excluded than have been to date. Furthermore, more schools might have been tempted to opt for grant maintained status and then later introduce selective criteria for entrance, than have done so as yet.

Explanations of exclusion based on family circumstances and dynamics

There are a wide range of debates and traditions upon which to draw when focusing upon family-based explanations of children's behaviour and ultimately their exclusion from school. The most useful focus might be the capacity of the family to take the lead in the primary socialization process. It is a focus which is often open to highly ideological assertions and interpretations of data (Havas 1995). Analysis might include the socio-economic circumstances of the family, as well as interactions within the family. There are strong opposing viewpoints about the efficacy of the modern family in relation to socializing the citizens of the future. On the Right some of the concerns are explicitly moral and economic, and in the case of Murray (1990) relate clearly to a desire to reduce welfare provision and his particular concept of 'underclass'. Murray's arguments could be criticized for the 'victim blaming' approach noted by Blyth and Milner (1994) in relation to school exclusions. However, other writers focus upon structural causes of underclass, such as Field (1990) and others still (such as Westergaard 1992) question the validity of the concept and usage of the term 'underclass'.

There are clearly differences within groups referred to as an underclass; the evidence that such a grouping reproduces itself, via the family, from one generation to the next is in question. Processes of youth transition and forms of social exclusion, whereby groups and individuals may be likely to follow a particular trajectory, without support or intervention, may be a more fruitful line of enquiry. Decisions about schooling (including SEN provision, exclusion from school and truancy) are one particular mechanism by which young people may be socially excluded. By shifting the focus towards routes to social exclusion the possibilities for intervention and diversion from this eventuality might be explored. The possibilities offered by family support should not be discounted, but this cannot be relied upon for all children and young people.

In contrast to Murray's implicit criticism of families, particularly single-parent families, Young and Halsey (1995) take an explicitly socialist view and focus upon the plight of children, which they view as posing the most serious social problem of our time. They liken the changes in the circumstances of children today to that of children in the early period of industrialization in the eighteenth and nineteenth centuries. In their view there has been a polarization of society in which the marginalization of some groups leaves many children in impoverished circumstances. However, Young and Halsey (1995: 10) add to the group of materially impoverished youngsters, those whom they see as suffering from 'time-poverty'. They point out that people who are successful in the modern economy make themselves the slaves of the clock, and even when they are physically present with their children 'they have no time for the moment in which children live'. This type of analysis is flexible enough to include families from a wide range of socio-economic circumstances.

Another type of analysis may be of utility here, that is the concept of the 'chaotic family'. This is a concept known to family therapists, social workers, psychiatrists and other mental health professionals (Barker 1993). It looks into the family as a system and analyses how it functions. In this respect it can be seen as based upon a somewhat conservative philosophy – the wider issues about power and control between the sexes and generations and in society as a whole are not fully considered. This concept is based on different models of control in families, which are termed: flexible, rigid, laissez-faire and chaotic. Control is referred to as the process by which family members influence each other, in order to establish and maintain order within the family system. Control is viewed as needed in order to make basic maintenance possible in families as well as to provide a structure within which adaptation to changing circumstances and new demands is possible. Barker (1993) quotes Steinhauer *et al.* (1984) in making the assessment that flexible styles of behavioural control are those most often found in healthily functioning families. Such styles are predictable but constructive and change in appropriate ways in response to changing circumstances. Rigid styles of behavioural control are high in predictability but low in constructiveness and adaptability. Laissez-faire styles of behavioural control combine moderate predictability with low constructiveness. Chaotic styles of control are low in both predictability and constructiveness. At times the style is laissez-faire and at others rigid.

One of the key aspects of such an analysis is based on learning theory and the modelling process by which children acquire social skills. If parents behave inconsistently children are likely to do so also. Barker (1993: 112) concludes: 'Children growing up in such families are at risk in many ways. Secure emotional attachments to their parents may not develop, their learning of social skills may be impaired and they may not learn to trust the adult world, and they may grow up with feelings of doubt about their worth.' Such an analysis is attractive in its identification of the location of a problem which can be worked upon. The ideas behind such an analysis may also be transferable to the behaviour of teachers in the classroom. However, as Ronen (1993) argues, there are a very wide range of techniques used for working with children and adolescents displaying behaviour problems (she writes of over 230 different types of technique currently in use) and although many of these involve work with parents, other techniques focus upon the individual. In some cases, of course, the child does not live with parents and an individual focus may become essential.

Individual-based explanations of exclusion

Individual-based explanations tend to be associated with medical and psychiatric models of behaviour. Occasionally, too, they may be aligned to the comments of moralists on the Right. Peagram (1993) has written of 'the original sin' model of explaining children's behaviour as drawing upon the Judaic/Christian belief systems as well as commonsense understandings sustained by them. In such explanations the behaviour of some children may be viewed as inherently 'bad' or even 'evil', as though it is an in-built attribute of the child, for which they (and their parents) are personally responsible.

Medical explanations of children's behaviour have tended to regard children as 'sick' and in need of treatment if they do not behave within some predefined range (Laslett 1983). Psychiatric disorder explanations of behaviour relate to medical explanations in many ways, many such explanations having developed out of the work of Rutter *et al.* (1970, 1975). However, as Peagram (1993) has noted, the very high prevalence rates of psychiatric disorder in children and adolescents have tended to indicate that traditional resources would be overwhelmed if all such children were referred for 'treatment'. Peagram views the shift in focus from individual to institution-based explanations of behaviour as partly a reaction to these prevalence studies.

There is in the 1990s, as Cooper (1994a) observes, a growing interest in attention deficit disorders, with or without hyperactivity (ADD, ADHD) in Britain. This is a psychiatric diagnosis rooted in theories associating behavioural difficulties with neurological dysfunction. This diagnosis is most often associated with treatment that involves drug and behavioural therapy. Ideus (1994) provides a sociological analysis of the cultural foundations of ADHD, in which she concedes that there is evidence that ADHD is likely to be rooted in the biology of the individual, but that the 'condition' is nevertheless a socially constructed mental health disorder. She raises important issues for consideration in relation to the impact of thus labelling children and makes the following observation:

> To label a 7 year old as mentally disordered believing the condition will magically disappear at the onset of puberty is a qualitatively different act than labelling a 7 year old as mentally disordered for a lifetime. A passing problem of childhood attention or inability to sit in a class is more easily discarded as part of one's core identity than is an incurable,

chronic 'handicapping condition,' even if this latter entitles one to special services in education or the workplace.

(Ideus 1994: 189)

Ideus thus introduces a note of caution about the possible consequences of a readiness to apply a particular label to an individual when trying to provide an explanation of why a child behaves in a particular way.

Emotional and behavioural difficulties, or EBD, is the terminology used within the educational service to refer to children whose behaviour is so problematic that they are viewed as having a special educational need. As with other types of SEN, schools are expected to cope with and provide for EBD within their allocated resources, unless the child is statemented. A statement carries with it additional resources to help address the child's identified needs within the school context. Cooper (1994b) suggests the most useful way of viewing EBD is a flexible one; he is against defining EBD as a 'within-child' or individual problem or as an environmentally produced phenomenon. Cooper acknowledges that in some cases individuals said to have ADHD, for example, may respond well to drugs treatment. Other children may modify their behaviour in response to clear, consistent and rewarding behaviour management approaches in schools and at home.

Summary and conclusions

This chapter set out by painting a broad picture of the context in which changes have occurred in the education system, changes which have been conceptualized as amounting to a quasi-market in education. It has attempted to explain this development and evaluate existing evidence about the likely effects of quasi-markets upon the education service, and specifically school exclusion. The chapter has provided a framework within which schools, families and individuals operate. In each of these areas there are other explanations available about why there are increased levels of recorded exclusion. It concludes that exclusion from school occurs in a complex set of interacting circumstances of which quasi-markets in education are an important feature.

The field research has tried to capture some of this complexity by taking into account not only the features which relate to the individual child (the within-child factors) but also their environment. 'Environment' is conceived of as primarily including the child's home and school environment. 'Environment' is also taken to include social policy factors which are likely to enhance or inhibit a child's chances of behaving in a way (and their chances of being responded to in a way) which will make it possible for them to stay in a school. Section 2 will present research evidence and consider how exclusion from primary school can be explained. But first Chapter 2 will present an overview of research which has been conducted on school exclusions.

Two

Research about exclusion from school

Background

Research about school exclusion may be viewed as developing out of the numerous studies and commentaries about the school-based behaviour of children and young people, which Galloway *et al.* (1982) and Lawrence *et al.* (1984) trace throughout this century and long before. Exclusion from school also relates in many ways to the prevalence studies referred to in the last chapter (see for example Rutter *et al.* 1970, 1975) as well as studies of changes in special educational provision (see for example, Lloyd-Smith 1984). Galloway *et al.* (1982: 1) remind us that: 'There is nothing new about violent and disruptive behaviour in schools. In the last century Charles Dickens publicised the educational standards at some independent schools in Nicholas Nickleby. At other, more well-known schools riots by pupils led to intervention by the army.' Such responses to 'riots' may have brought order to a particular situation, but there is no evidence that the availability of such measures could prevent problems arising in the first place. Lawrence *et al.* (1984) confirm this and observe that canings and beatings were the only way that some level of order was maintained in schools in the past. Lawrence *et al.* (p. 8) point to Erasmus's preference for removing from school, rather than punishing 'dull or worthless boys', as a forerunner of exclusion.

A number of small scale studies were undertaken into exclusion during the 1970s and 1980s, such as York *et al.* (1972), Grunsell (1979) and that of Galloway *et al.* (1982), Gale and Topping (1986), McLean (1987), McManus (1987), and Franklyn-Stokes (1989). These studies provide some local statistics, characteristics of the children involved, as well as the reasons given by head teachers for the exclusion. In some cases the patterns in terms of rate of exclusion and school characteristics and organization are identified and analysed. Research on exclusions has usually focused upon the more numerous secondary school pupils, although York *et al.* (1972) included both primary and secondary age pupils in their study. In the early 1980s Galloway *et al.* (1982: xiv) argued that 'very few pupils are ever suspended from primary schools following disruptive behaviour . . . they can be transferred to a special school before suspension becomes necessary.'

The possible association between special educational needs and exclusion, made explicit by Galloway *et al.* (1982), is a theme which will be pursued later in this chapter. The extreme rarity of records of primary school exclusions until the 1990s has meant that it has not been the focus of published research to date, with the exception of Parsons *et al.* (1994) and Hayden (1994). Exclusion from primary school has not been the main concern in any of the large scale surveys undertaken. Where young children have been included in more localized research they are generally incorporated as part of an investigation which also includes older, secondary age pupils.

National surveys conducted or commissioned by government departments have been more recent. In the early 1980s, Galloway *et al.* (1982) noted a reluctance, on the part of government, to conduct and publicize surveys on the issue. They surmised that this was because of political sensitivity about exclusion. In 1990 the DfE began the first official effort to collect information systematically and nationally, over a two-year period (Lovey *et al.* 1993).

Numbers, trends and characteristics

There is now evidence from a variety of reliable sources of a significant growth in the number of officially recorded exclusions during the first half of the 1990s. All of the surveys conducted have been concerned with identifying and confirming trends in the number of exclusions recorded and, where possible, producing a national estimate in a given time period. However, it must be considered that there are no comparative national data for an earlier period and it is worth considering that some of the apparent 'increase' in exclusions may partly be a feature of better recording systems and fewer 'unofficial exclusions' (AEP 1992). On the other hand, researchers in the field such as Stirling (1991) point to the consistent underreporting of exclusions.

The evidence for this recorded rise in official exclusions comes from government departments in the form of the National Exclusions Reporting System (DfE 1992), the survey of Parsons *et al.* (1995) conducted for the DfE and the Office for Standards in Education (OFSTED 1993; Hofkins 1994); from unions and professional associations (AEP 1992; NUT 1992; SHA 1992; NAHT 1994); from market research organizations (MORI 1993); and from independent advisory bodies, such as the Advisory Centre for

Table 2.1 Estimates of numbers of permanent exclusions September 1990–July 1995 (government departments/commissioned research)

Year	All permanent exclusions	Primary only
1990–1	2,910	378
1991–2	3,833	537
1992–3	7,000–8,000	—
1993–4	11,181	1,297
1994–5	12,458	1,445

Source: 1990–2 DfE (1992); 1992–3 Hofkins (1994), refers to secondary age pupils only; 1993–4 and autumn 1994 Parsons *et al.* (1995); 1994–5 Parsons (1995), update on original sample.

Education (ACE 1993b). The key estimates of numbers of permanent exclusions, by or for government departments, are summarized in Table 2.1. The upward trend in official records of permanent exclusion is clear.

However, the SHA (1992) survey stressed how very unusual exclusion is when analysed as a percentage rate in a pupil population. In the SHA survey of over 800 secondary schools with 600,000 pupils, the survey found 2.4 per cent of all pupils experienced some form of exclusion in a school year and 0.21 per cent experienced a permanent exclusion. The rates were lower in voluntary aided and controlled schools, grant maintained and independent schools.

Parsons *et al.* (1995: 3) note that rates of permanent exclusion for the 1993–4 school year were 1 in 3,270, or 0.031 per cent of all primary age children, and 1 in 282, or 0.35 per cent of all secondary age children.

The NERS exercise (DfE 1992) produced the first national information available about the basic characteristics of excluded children. Most other surveys have not collected these data in a systematic way. Surveys have either related to the whole-school population or to secondary school children only.

The NERS showed exclusion to be a predominantly secondary school phenomenon, with 15 as the peak age for exclusion for both boys and girls. Exclusions in the primary phase accounted for 13 per cent of the total in year one (1990–1) and 14 per cent of the total in year two (1991–2). Parsons *et al.* (1995) have since found a slightly lower proportion but higher numbers of primary age children excluded from school in their national survey. According to the NERS, many more boys than girls were excluded; a ratio of 4 : 1 in year one and 5 : 1 in year two. The SHA (1992), Imich (1994) and Parsons *et al.* (1995) confirm the overrepresentation of boys in exclusion statistics, and it has been noted that this gender weighting becomes more marked with the more severe exclusions (SHA 1992). There has been relatively little commentary or analysis of the overrepresentation of boys in exclusion statistics. Franklyn-Stokes (1989) relates this overrepresentation to the broader issue of patterns of criminality and deviance, as has the SHA (1992) survey. Furlong (1985) suggests that evidence about deviance in schools would point to girls being equally disaffected, but that they tend to have different ways of expressing their disaffection. Franklyn-Stokes (1989) also suggests that teachers, especially male teachers, may be more tolerant of girls.

The NERS found that African-Caribbean pupils were disproportionately represented within the excluded pupil population: 8.1 per cent of the total in year one and 8.5 per cent of the total in year two. However, Parsons *et al.* (1995) did not include a question about ethnicity in their survey for the DfE. Despite the absence of reliable national data on the ethnicity of excluded pupils, the issue has attracted more attention than that of sex or age. A wide-ranging group of researchers and commentators have provided evidence on this issue (ACE 1992; Sasson 1993; Stirling 1993b; Bourne *et al.* 1994; Cohen *et al.* 1994; Gillborn 1995; as well as the CRE and some LEAs and a BBC documentary, 10 November 1994). Exclusion has been viewed as a direct result of institutional racism (Sasson 1993). Sasson also refers to anecdotal evidence that 'when white youngsters are turned off schools and the curriculum, they truant. Black youngsters are forced by their parents to go to school where they become disruptive and, in due course, expelled' (p. 111).

In more recent years the Chairman of the CRE has commented upon the low priority given to combating racism in schools. The Office for Standards in Education (OFSTED) is viewed as according racial equality a low priority in their school inspections. Other concerns have been voiced in a number of areas, such as the reduction of Section 11 (language support) funding, the low expectations of pupils from teachers, as well as the lack of teachers from Black and minority ethnic backgrounds (Pyke 1995). Some individual local authorities have made information on exclusion and ethnicity publicly available, occasionally in report form (see for example, NCCED 1989; Mayet 1992; Lamb 1993).

Bourne *et al.* (1994) explain this overrepresentation of Black children in exclusion statistics as part of the way they believe Black families are pathologized, and as part of a system of economic and social exclusion. Like the CRE they also point to the abandonment of anti-racist policies and the watering down of multicultural perspectives as a reason why racial prejudice may be resurfacing in schools. Bourne *et al.* locate exclusion in the longer-term debate about how Black children have been separated out from their White peers within the education system in saying: 'In sum, teacher expectations of black children as low achievers and a disciplinary problem, which once consigned them to ESN [educationally subnormal] schools and 'Sin-bins', today excludes them from a school altogether' (p. vi). The overlap in issues to do with ethnicity and definitions of what is now referred to as special educational need are important, in that children with special educational needs are overrepresented among cases of exclusion.

There has been a great deal of commentary about the vulnerability of children with special educational needs in a more market-led system, as well as an acknowledgement that there is an overrepresentation of children with special educational needs in the available exclusion statistics (for example Peagram 1991; Stirling 1992; Lovey *et al.* 1993; Bourne *et al.* 1994; Cohen *et al.* 1994). The NERS exercise showed that between six and seven times the expected number of children with statements had been permanently excluded over the two-year period of monitoring (12.5 per cent of the total in year one and 15 per cent in year two). Only about 2 per cent of the school population are likely to have a statement of special educational need at any one time, although another 18 per cent of children are likely to have a non-statemented special educational need at some time in their school career (Warnock 1978).

An ACE (1992) survey reported that the highest proportion of their calls about exclusion involved children with special educational needs. The ACE report states: 'Invariably, parents reported that the schools felt that they could no longer cope with the child' (p. 9). A document by the Special Educational Consortium (1993) suggests that as only 29 per cent of the permanent exclusions in the DfE study (first year) returned to mainstream school in the first instance after their permanent exclusion, it follows that 71 per cent of the children permanently excluded had some sort of 'special provision', which as the DfE discussion paper acknowledges, did not always meet the child's needs. The Special Educational Consortium (p. 5) state that 'An excluded child should, almost by definition, have some sort of emotional and behavioural or learning difficulty. If the difficulty is not with the child, then it is with the school and questions must be raised about the effective management of that school.' AMA (1995) research notes the difficulty of protecting special needs support both within and outside schools, under a system of local management of schools. The AMA press release states that 'Support services have got to be given mandatory exception from the local management scheme. LEAs have got to have the power to make sure those with special needs get the education they require.' Peagram (1991), Stirling (1992) and Mayet (1992) have all noted the particular vulnerability to exclusion of children with emotional and behavioural difficulties, which the AMA (1995) report appears to confirm.

Reasons for exclusions

Physical aggression has been a significant factor in research investigating the reasons for exclusion. NERS found this to be a factor in over a quarter of cases, Imich (1994) in nearly a third of cases and Islington Education Department (Lamb 1993) in over half of cases. Generally disruptive or 'unacceptable' behaviour tends to be the next most common reason, followed by verbal abuse to staff and other pupils. In a minority of cases, drugs, vandalism/arson and theft have been shown to feature in cases of exclusion. Blythe and Milner (1993) have raised the issue that such reasons, though showing a fairly consistent pattern across much of the research conducted, are as recorded reasons by definition the *official* reasons provided by the head teacher, and as such should be treated with caution. They suggest that in reality, the formal reason given for an exclusion is likely to represent 'the final straw' after a long period of difficult relationships and incidents within a school; the work of Galloway *et al.* (1982) is used to support this suggestion. This culmination of events, they point out, might explain the apparent triviality of particular instances which have been reported as triggering a specific exclusion, such as 'repeated failure to abide by the school rules concerning length of hair' (BBC, 15 March 1993) and 'disruptive' behaviour (Channel 4, 2 March 1993).

Most of the surveys have addressed themselves to uncovering the underlying reasons for the recorded increase in exclusions, which usually relate to the effects of quasi-markets in education. The NERS recognized what it referred to as incentives and disincentives for schools to exclude a pupil, which relate largely to funding and whether or not schools should be expected to make their exclusion rates publicly available. The increased competition between schools generated by open enrolment and the publication of league tables of exam results and truancy rates has been cited in most national surveys, such as AEP (1992), NUT (1992) and MORI (1993). Some surveys have also emphasized the stress and pressure on schools arising from the changes brought about by the 1988 Act and since (NCCED 1989; AEP 1992; NUT 1992).

The reduction in the power of LEAs and in particular the support services they are able to provide, specifically educational psychologist time, are also often cited as key underlying reasons (Stirling 1991; AEP 1992; NUT 1992; MORI 1993). The NUT (1992) survey actually found that the 27 LEAs responding to them placed resource issues at the top of the list of underlying reasons for increases in exclusions. The reported shortfalls in resources were manifest in a number of ways: in the demands of delivering the full requirements of the National Curriculum with the accompanying testing and assessment arrangements; in the lack of alternative provision for children perceived as in need of it; and in the lack of educational psychologist time and support services to address behaviour problems.

As already indicated, the NERS exercise showed a clear overrepresentation of children with statements in recorded permanent exclusions. Stirling (1993a) describes the reality of the options open to schools when faced with a child whose behaviour suggests that they may have special educational needs and in effect cannot be taught in a full class without additional support. A school can attempt to access additional resources via the often lengthy formal assessment and statementing process (meanwhile the child's behaviour is likely to be deteriorating further), or they can resort to the much more immediate option of exclusion. While Stirling has found that most schools in practice prefer to explore the first option, she notes the disincentives in terms of time and money in doing so. Meanwhile it is likely that parents of other children in this child's class will be complaining, and may be even threatening to take their children elsewhere, with the associated financial consequences for the school.

However, it must also be considered that not all excluded children fall into the category of having identified or possible special educational need. Poor behaviour and indiscipline are also a factor in the view of some commentators. There has been an expression of concern by teachers that a minority of children are presenting with more difficult behaviour and at a younger age (Lawrence and Steed 1986; Coxon 1988; TES 1991). This concern was reflected in the Elton Report on discipline in schools (DES/WO 1989). Rutter (1991) and Rutter and Smith (1995) argue the case that there is evidence of increased incidence of child psychiatric disorder. The high incidence of persistence in 'disorders' diagnosed early is noted, especially with boys. Persistence is apparently more likely in the case of conduct disorders and emotional disorders. Rutter (1991) refers to the great range of contributing social factors (e.g. increasing relative poverty, unemployment and family breakdown) which are likely to affect more children adversely in our own time than in the recent past. He concludes that the greatest chance of a positive change for these individuals relates to improvements in family circumstances, peer group relationships and those with significant others and 'good school experiences'. In a more recent study, Rutter and Smith (1995) concede that there is no simple relationship between 'psychosocial disorders' and relative deprivation, but they do note that the trend towards a more individualistic ethos in society and the push to succeed may have added to the pressures on young people.

The frustration of the teaching profession faced with the everyday realities of difficult behaviour, whether or not it is a symptom of social or educational need, or indeed psychiatric disturbance is encapsulated in this quote from the NAHT (1994: 2) which stresses the issue of order and discipline in the following press release, following their survey into exclusions:

> Many parents have abrogated their responsibilities and their children are out of control. Heads and their staff are heartily sick of being held responsible for the consequences of what is clearly a breakdown of discipline in society. The government must change its policy or be found guilty of abandoning its responsibility to give schools full support in maintaining order and discipline.

The NAHT want a reinstatement of the indefinite exclusion option, which they see as a possible reason for further increases in permanent exclusions since September 1994. This last point relates to wider issues about the range of disciplinary options open to schools trying to address unwanted behaviour. A perceived gap in the range of measures left by the abolition of corporal punishment in 1986 is part of this reduction in options.

A more general hardening of attitudes within the teaching profession has been noted by some commentators. For example the AMA (1995) has observed what they describe as a 'lowering of the threshold in the tolerance of aberrant behaviour in schools'. Some social services staff have also seen an evaporation in sympathy for what they have referred to as 'problem' children. Lineham (1994: 7) has quoted social services staff as saying: 'There is very little understanding or wish to sympathise with the fact that by their behaviour children are expressing things that have happened to them.' The article continues in its analysis: 'It is one of the cornerstones of "back to basics" that people misbehave because they are bad. In John Major's words, we need to understand less and condemn more.' This last quote harks back to the kind of 'original sin' model for explaining unwanted behaviour in children referred to in the last chapter.

Differences in rates of exclusion

The SHA (1992) survey noted another of the features about the growing evidence in the exclusion debate. The variation in numbers of exclusions across schools is an issue which greatly interests and encourages professionals concerned with supporting schools and facilitating the admission of excluded pupils to new schools (Robotham 1995). The work of Galloway (1982, 1985), McManus (1987) and McLean (1987) has already established these differences. For example, McManus (1987: 270), in reporting upon a study of 49 high schools in Leeds, concluded that: 'The results suggest that high rates of suspension reflect high bureaucratic involvement in pastoral care and discipline: suspensions are the unintended consequence of some procedures in some schools.' However, McManus points out that this study is concerned with a restricted aspect of school life and thus no inferences should be drawn about other important characteristics of a school, such as the academic performance of the pupils or the amount of disruptive behaviour. Thus absence of exclusion does not mean that there are no serious problems with certain individuals in low-excluding schools. Importantly, no evidence is presented of the effect (if any) on staff and pupils in schools which rarely or do not exclude. McLean (1987: 303) examined the exclusion rate in 57 secondary schools in Scotland and concluded that overall: 'Across the 57 schools, exclusion rates were significantly related to the amount of disadvantage in intake . . . [however] the schools seemed to have more influence over how many pupils they excluded than how often pupils attended or how well they did academically.' McLean nonetheless identified schools which bucked the trend, and found that six schools in particular, which could be described as low-excluding in disadvantaged areas, shared a child-centred ideology and a preventive approach to disruption.

The SHA (1992: 2) gave less credence to this sort of focus in their report, which says: 'Without doubt, much, if not most of this difference, as with examination results variation, relates to the nature of the intake of the school.' However, the report does go on to say: 'About two thirds of permanent exclusions come from a quarter of schools, and the ratio holds for LEA, GMS, and independent sectors. Large schools do not permanently exclude at a higher rate.' Both the SHA report and that of the NCCED (1989) found that behaviour in schools is good on the whole. The NCCED report indicates that there is little connection between the likelihood that a discipline issue would end in exclusion and whether or not the school had a discipline policy.) The NCCED team found that most difficulties over poor behaviour were rooted in day-to-day classroom interaction, not in poor policies.) Some of the work set was inappropriate for the ability of the pupils. Difficulties were particularly prevalent in lessons provided by supply teachers who have less knowledge of the group they are expected to teach; over half of their lessons were thwarted by disruption (Cohen *et al.* 1994).

The family perspective

There has been a relatively limited amount of published research which has investigated the family circumstances and background of excluded children. Cohen *et al.* (1994) present material about families drawn from 30 cases submitted by workers at Barnado's projects and from family service units. Both are voluntary agencies providing social welfare services to children and families experiencing difficulties of various kinds; difficulties which the authors describe as often relating to poverty, disadvantage and discrimination. Thus this study is very much focused upon excluded children from family circumstances where there are already acknowledged difficulties. The study is therefore concentrated upon a particularly disadvantaged subgroup of excluded children.

The characteristics and circumstances of these children are an accentuated version of some of the trends shown by the NERS exercise. Thus, nearly half of the children were reported to have special educational needs and the great majority of families were on income support. Most of the children were boys, and nearly half the children were of primary school age. Nearly a third of the children were from Black, mixed-race or from minority ethnic backgrounds. The reasons given by schools for exclusion also reflect other studies, although again there appears to be a concentration on the more serious categories of event. Cohen *et al.* (1994: 33) state:

> in almost all cases, the exclusion was reported to be the result of 'violent, disruptive or unmanageable behaviour', which was often said to have gone on for some time. On occasions, the issue was restricted to verbal aggression, but in some instances, the behaviour described was severe – alleged sexual attack on another pupil, or serious assaults on staff or other pupils.

One such assault involved allegations of rape and stabbing. Cohen *et al.* describe how there was generally a high degree of contact between parent and school before the exclusion, although such contact was not always harmonious. Nevertheless a particular exclusion event could still seem sudden and was clearly likely to compound any existing difficulties in home–school relations. Most parents, in line with other studies (ACE 1992; DfE 1992) did not consider an appeal, largely through lack of knowledge of legal procedures but also because they felt it would be pointless.

Cohen *et al.* (1994) show increasing interpersonal and personal difficulties within families, attributed as a result of the exclusion. A minority of children were accommodated by the local authority, some children displayed self-destructive and delinquent behaviour. There were also problems reported between the excluded individual and their parent(s) and sibling(s). Some families highlighted the extra expense created for them by exclusion, both because of the loss of free school meals and the need to try and make some compensation for the lack of activities and stimulus for the child while they were out of school. Furthermore, babysitting costs were incurred in some families. Some of the parents reported feeling blamed for their children's behaviour which they also said they found hard to contain. The children were often out of school for long periods, with half of them missing at least six months of schooling and two children being out of school for three years or more. They usually had little or no input from home tuition or other education support services.

The findings of Parsons *et al.* (1994) are consistent with those of Cohen *et al.*; Parsons *et al.* conducted in-depth research into 11 primary age children excluded from school in three different LEAs. These children were all boys and all but one had been permanently excluded from school. Thus, although these case studies come from a wider setting than families using the services of Barnado's and family service units, they are still the extreme end of the spectrum in terms of the severity of the type of exclusion. Parsons *et al.* (p. 27) summarize the family circumstances of the 11 excluded children in the following way: 'Eight of the children live in families which face problems of the sort Barker (1993) describes in the "chaotic" family. Social services are providing support in six of these families.'

Parsons *et al.* (1994) describe the experience of exclusion as usually shocking and sometimes devastating for both pupil and parents. This study points to the important issues of the deinstitutionalizing effect of permanent exclusion on a young child and the isolation of a child from their friends and wider community. In addition the seemingly individual and personal nature of exclusion is highlighted. Some of the parents interviewed saw the exclusion as a result of a personality clash between the child and teacher and on occasion between themselves and the head teacher.

Within the research on exclusion and even specifically that on families, there is relatively little direct evidence of investigation and reporting upon the child's experience, especially when the children are of primary age. Parsons *et al.* included interviews with children in their study but do not report upon these interviews in detail separately. There are some accounts of exclusion from secondary age pupils, such as that of Galloway *et al.* (1982: 54), who found the pupils interviewed to be 'a peculiarly vulnerable group'. Franklyn-Stokes (1989) included interviews in her study of secondary age pupils. She found that pupils who perceived themselves to be different from their peers at the age of 11 were significantly more likely to be excluded subsequently. Pupils' explanations for their exclusions were also related to these perceptions of sameness or difference at age 11. Gersch and Nolan (1994) have focused on the issue of what children think about exclusion in their study of six pupils attending a London borough's special provision for excluded pupils. This study reveals early difficulties in primary school with respect to both learning and behaviour, as well as peer relations. Pupils reported that they had other worries at the time of their exclusion, worries which most often related to their family circumstances. Importantly, five of the six children said that they wanted a fresh start, although they were worried about getting on with other pupils in a new school.

Marks (1995) concentrated upon a small group of 12 and 13-year-olds in her analysis of pupils' experiences of the process of exclusion. Marks (p. 97) concludes from her interviews with the children that 'their sense of self was often intimately bound up with the experience of exclusion'.

The role of agencies outside school

Both Cohen *et al.* (1994) and Parsons *et al.* (1994) found a high incidence of families involved with a wide range of agencies outside schools. Many because of their special educational needs had been through, or were going through, the multi-agency process of assessment, involving education, health and often social services professionals. In addition families were already receiving support for their own difficulties, in all cases, according to the research carried out by Cohen *et al.*, and in over half of the cases investigated by Parsons *et al.* The involvement of other agencies with families of excluded children, in particular social services departments, has been noted by Stirling (1992) and reported upon in *Community Care* on a number of occasions (such as Cohen 1994). It has been asserted by Stirling (1992) that exclusion is likely to increase the level of involvement of social services in the lives of some families, and as already indicated, may even help precipitate children being looked after by the local authority. Both Cohen *et al.* (1994) and Parsons *et al.* (1994) show an increase in the need for social services support in some of their case studies.

Normington (1994) highlights the lengthy and highly documented conflicts between social services departments and education departments, a conflict which she describes as often explained in terms of differences in personality, training and perspective – the social work focus being on the individual, and that of the teacher being on the group, the class, the year group and the whole school. However, she and others view these differences as valuable in terms of what they might offer to a child and as not insurmountable in terms of working together in the interests of a child. Collaboration rarely occurs for children 'looked after' by the local authority. A report on the education of 'looked-after' children shows insufficient planning and liaison between social workers, carers and teachers, for these children (DoH/OFSTED 1995). The report also notes the high proportion of children who had a history of poor attendance or exclusion from school, although this was more marked with older children (14 to 16-year-olds).

The effects of exclusion

Parsons *et al.* (1994), Cohen *et al.* (1994) and Gersch and Nolan (1994) all supply some sense of the immediate effects of exclusion in their accounts from the point of view of families, and children. Parsons *et al.* (1994: 75) describe the permanent exclusion of primary school children in the following way:

> The point of exclusion is an explosive event. The child is ejected from school. There is no organised transition from one form of institutional provision to another. The effect of this on the child, a child who is usually in the state of being unable to control his own behaviour, is inevitably damaging. The manner in which the exclusion occurs means that there are increased difficulties for follow-up services to deal with including stressed families and children whose self-esteem is further damaged.

Parsons *et al.* go on to explain what they refer to as the 'debris management' of the child and family after such an event, a process which they describe as slow and difficult, particularly because of the lack of intervention, support and planning which preceded the event. Families enter into a situation which has been described as a 'policy vacuum' by Lloyd-Smith (1993), where there are no automatic systems or structures available to offer immediate support and alternatives, in a situation which amounts to a crisis for many families.

There has been relatively slight reference in research to date as to whether the increasing use of exclusions as a sanction by schools has any positive effects on the individual pupil's behaviour and that of others in the school. Gale and Topping (1986) concluded that exclusion was unlikely to have a positive effect on subsequent behaviour. Imich (1994) notes the likelihood of a reduction in the impact of exclusion as a punishment as they become more common. He also raises the possibility that exclusion may be viewed as a rewarding experience by some children and in effect something to aim for, a point also made by Blyth and Milner (1996) in relation to secondary age pupils and alternative educational provision.

York *et al.* (1972) conducted a limited follow-up study a little over a year after their original research involving 41 excluded children in the city of Edinburgh (one to three years after the children's exclusions). The follow-up study included 25 children who were still at school: 'While at the time of the exclusion only one child was not living at home, at the time of the follow-up 21 children were living in residential care of some kind. In a more structured environment away from family stresses, these children were now contained in school' (York *et al.* 1972: 265–6). These residential facilities included psychiatric hospitals, residential schools and children's homes. York *et al.* conclude that the exclusions did not occur as the result of an arbitrary decision by a teacher and that the prognosis for the children was very poor. In contrast Franklyn-Stokes (1989) found that the majority of excluded pupils in her study (secondary age) returned to their schools and presented few, if any further problems. The minority of pupils who left mainstream education had more limited options, which Franklyn-Stokes (p. 46) describes as 'a variety of holding operations' until they reached school-leaving age. The marked difference between these two prognoses might be explained in part by the types of exclusion investigated, as well as the source and size of the sample studied. York *et al.* (1972) obtained some of their sample (ten children) from children already attending a child guidance centre, the rest of the children being permanently excluded. The sample of York *et al.* included more extreme cases, while that of Franklyn-Stokes (1989) included all types of secondary school exclusion in a year in one local authority.

There are likely to be increasing numbers of children outside the school system for periods, in that there is evidence emerging of head teachers being increasingly reluctant to take on children excluded from other schools (NUT 1992; SHA 1992; Stirling 1992). LEAs do have the power to direct a school with spare capacity to take in a child excluded from elsewhere but the very need to have to direct a school does not bode well for the acceptance of the child. Furthermore LEAs are likely to have more difficulty getting accurate information from schools outside local authority control. As the SHA (1992: 4) survey comments: 'The rate of admissions of excluded pupils [to other schools] declines steeply as ties with LEAs become weaker.' Importantly the SHA survey found a discrepancy between the numbers of children permanently excluded from school and the numbers of such children re-entering the school system. The SHA acknowledge that some of this discrepancy may be to do with systems of recording, but nevertheless some pupils may be in effect 'lost' from the education system.

Discussion about the longer-term effects of exclusion is perhaps usefully informed by much longer-running debates about the adverse effects of children missing school through truancy and other forms of non-attendance (such as Graham 1988; Carlen *et al.* 1992; O'Keeffe 1994), which official statistics show to be a much bigger problem than exclusion. Also research in the field of juvenile delinquency has made clear links between certain aspects of school behaviour, such as truancy, 'troublesomeness', dishonesty, aggressiveness and bullying, and later delinquency (Farrington 1980). The prevalence and visibility of these behaviours has been associated with the kind of work referred to earlier which focuses on school ethos (e.g. Rutter *et al.* 1979; Graham 1988). There have been some explicit attempts in the media to link the issue of exclusion with delinquency (e.g. BBC *Panorama*, 15 March 1993; Pyke 1993). However, any link between exclusion and delinquency is likely to be complex; children known to be displaying problematic behaviour at home and in the community do not necessarily also get excluded from school (Hayden 1994). Furthermore, the great majority of exclusions are only for a matter of a few school days, time periods which may seem fairly insignificant in comparison with school holidays, weekends or indeed the end of the school day, as periods of time in which there is the possibility of anti-social behaviour, when children are not adequately supervised.

A crucial difference between exclusion and non-attendance, however, is the fact that the individuals and families concerned lose the right of access to school-based education, a very basic service and expectation in civilized society. It can be argued that exclusion does not remove the right to education in that there is an alternative service in the form of EOTAS (education other than at school), which may take a number of forms such as home tuition or PRUs (pupil referral units). However, such provisions do not amount to full-time education nor full access to what has been termed the 'entitlement' of the National Curriculum: individuals in receipt of EOTAS can be disapplied from such an entitlement. Available information about the quality of such provisions suggests that it is variable, often part-time in what is offered and under threat of reduction in service or even closure (Blyth and Milner 1993; Lovey *et al.* 1993; OFSTED 1993, 1995).

Concerns are emerging that exclusion may place children at risk in a number of ways, one of which is the increased likelihood of being taken into local authority care, as already indicated (Stirling 1992; Parsons *et al.* 1994). This factor alone is known to be associated with poor educational outcomes for the child concerned. Blyth and Milner (1993) extend this debate to consider the process of marginalization of groups within the population and their existence outside mainstream society, an effect which has been referred to as social exclusion. It has been argued that social exclusion is demonstrated by a constellation of disadvantage and inequality including high unemployment, dependency on state benefits and services, poverty, poor housing, debt, police and welfare surveillance (see for example, Lockwood 1985). Permanent exclusion of a child from school may provide one of the entry points to this marginalized way of life.

Discussion

There is evidence that children have always been excluded from school and that some children have not attended school regularly, for a variety of reasons (ACE 1993a). However, research evidence shows a clear increase in official records of exclusion over the 1990–5 period. Viewpoints about why (and whether) this should happen are varied. For example, Sivandan, Director of the Institute of Race Relations, provides a thought-provoking comment in the introduction to Bourne *et al.* (1994: v):

Exclusion is seldom the measure of a child's capacity to learn; it is an indication, instead, of the teacher's refusal to be challenged. And, when you have an education system which puts a premium not on the educability of the child but on the price of its education, the challenge to the teacher is the financial cost of keeping it in school, not the human cost of keeping it out. When, in addition, educability itself is prejudged in terms of a societal stereotype which associates 'black' with 'problem', the exclusion of the black child becomes that much more automatic.

This may be seen as perhaps a particularly emotive viewpoint about why exclusion is happening in the current education system: exclusion as a symptom of a power struggle between adults and children, a consequence of a market-based system in education, as well as a result of the specific issue of racism. Exclusion certainly raises the issue of whether children and parents can expect a right of access to school-based education, as opposed to part-time alternatives outside the school system, such as home tuition or pupil referral units. It is clear at the moment that there is no right of access to a school-based education for everybody. In fact some commentators have questioned the notion of any right to education, as this quote from the head teacher of a grant maintained school illustrates (Beckett 1992: 127):

This government's thrust since 1979 has been to give parents more responsibility. At this school we have responded to the mood of the government and what it seeks to do. Residual bits of the 1944 Education Act make this more complicated. This Act should be changed to make parents completely responsible in law as well as morally . . . Parents alone should be responsible for finding school places. If they fail to co-operate properly with the school, and cause their children to be expelled, their children should not be educated.

The idea that some children could be denied education is a shocking one, but one which is in effect already a reality for some children, in relation to school-based education or an equivalent. Parsons et al. (1994) and Hayden (1994) have already shown that primary age children can be out of school for months and occasionally years, through the lack of alternatives to school-based education in some localities. Thus exclusion in the 1990s differs from periods before the Education Reform Act 1988 because of a whole range of changes in the way the education system operates and the relatively low priority given to children who make extra demands on the system. Chapter 1 describes these changes as adding up to a 'quasi-market' in education. In particular, the extra fragmentation of the education system created by the introduction of grant maintained schools and city technology colleges adds to the existing difficulties with voluntary aided and special agreement schools. All of these types of school are in a good position to resist any approach from the LEA to admit a pupil excluded from elsewhere. Parents do have the right of appeal and LEA officers may assist them in this, but the reality is that such procedures are very time consuming and uncertain of success. Sasson (1992: 92), an education officer in Brent, describes the situation in LEA schools in the following way: 'When it comes to County schools, the situation does not become much better. Popular County schools, anyway, are full to overflowing. Less popular ones are determined to improve their image and will resist tooth and nail accepting pupils who are likely to disrupt the smooth functioning of their institutions.' Sasson recognizes additional problems created by the drive to reduce spare school places as well as the particular difficulty of finding a space in a school with places in suitable option groups for 15 and 16-year-olds who are already studying for GCSEs.

At the heart of the debate about exclusion is the behaviour of children in school and what is considered acceptable and unacceptable behaviour in a particular school. Therefore while many teachers might agree that 'exclusion is seldom the measure of a child's capacity to learn', they may add that it is an indication that the exclusion of a particular child might enhance the learning opportunities of other children, as well as the ability of the teacher to do their job effectively. Exclusion also highlights the issue of the boundaries between the responsibility of parents and that of schools in ensuring appropriate behaviour during the school day. However, as Rollinson (1990) points out, the great majority of teachers have not been equipped during their training to deal with the behaviours they are occasionally faced with, largely because serious behaviour problems are relatively rare in mainstream classrooms. As numerous reports from OFSTED (and before them HMI) emphasize, most schools and classrooms are orderly places most of the time and the great majority of pupils respond to what may be termed 'normal' adult discipline. In fact one report from OFSTED has asserted that discipline in most schools has not declined although exclusions have increased (*Education* 1993b). In effect OFSTED are emphasizing schools' responsibility in making the decision to exclude, rather than tolerate or attempt to deal with the behaviour viewed as 'unacceptable'.

In many ways, however, the broad explanations and categorizations utilized in research and debate about school exclusion are revisiting well-known debates in the sociology of education, a field of study which has had a strong tradition of explaining the way inequalities in society are reproduced. There has been analysis of the education policy framework which is helping to make exclusion a logical option for schools, as well as reference to the broad social trends which may be leading to greater stress within families. It is acknowledged that stress in families may then be manifest in the behaviour some children display when they are in school. It is also clear from this research that exclusion is not, however, an inevitable consequence of these policies and social trends. It has been demonstrated that schools do exclude at differential rates, even taking into account the differences in socio-economic circumstances of pupils across schools. It is noted that some individual head teachers are taking a stand and openly declare that they will not exclude a pupil from their school. However, this does not then mean that such schools expect to deal with children excluded from other schools. Schools which do exclude, on the other hand, are expecting another school to cope with what they could or would not. Yet certain types of school are in a better position to resist the approaches of the LEA and the families/carers of permanently excluded children. It is the duty of the LEA to educate a child, although not necessarily in a school. In this context children are likely to be out of school for longer periods than in the past, because it is becoming more difficult to secure another school place in an increasingly fragmented education system. This latter change relates directly to the government's express purpose of increasing the 'diversity' of educational provision in the context of a 'quasi-market' in education. The resistance among head teachers to taking on children who have been excluded from other schools can also be attributed to the introduction of quasi-markets in education on several counts: in relation to funding arrangements for such individuals, which are often perceived to be inadequate; in relation to the image and marketability of the school and the pressures from other parents as 'customers'; and in relation to the possible effects on the achievements of other children and thus measurable outputs in terms of academic results.

Summary and conclusions

Research about exclusions has provided wide-ranging evidence to support what appears to be a very real increase in the phenomenon. There is broad agreement about the characteristics of the pupils most vulnerable to this event. Several important gaps have been identified in the information available about exclusions. Primarily there is a lack of research, with the exception of Parsons *et al.* (1994), which focuses specifically upon primary age children. It has yet to be fully considered whether primary school exclusions may have a different function and meaning from exclusions in the secondary phase. Evidence available is concentrated on a small number of the most problematic cases. There is a need, through the careful corroborating of evidence at a number of levels, to investigate how the wider range of primary age pupils, who experience perhaps only a fixed term exclusion, fits into the picture. For example, is a fixed term exclusion a very different type of event from a permanent exclusion, or is it a forerunner or warning of the more serious event of permanent exclusion? More generally, exclusions research tends to focus upon groups of pupils most overrepresented in exclusion statistics, which means that some important although obvious points are overlooked. The most obvious of these is the fact that official records of exclusion suggest that most excluded pupils do not have a statement of special educational need and they are usually White. Excluded girls have largely been ignored in most research. Also the tendency is to focus upon the more economically and socially disadvantaged families and home circumstances. What of the more affluent children who are excluded from school?

Available research to date on primary school exclusions does not analyse the perspectives of both class and head teachers, yet these individuals have very different roles and responsibilities in respect of exclusion. Attempts to investigate fully precisely what behaviours primary age children are displaying, which are then deemed to warrant exclusion, have been limited. There is a need to cross-reference the evidence in relation to the context in which such behaviours are displayed, such as in the classroom, at lunchtimes and breaks; or everywhere, including home and community. There have been no thorough investigations of the circumstances at home and in school at the time of the exclusion event(s). There has been no clear analysis, of what parents/carers and schools are asking of each other in relation to excluded children, nor of the extent to which, in a particular exclusion event, there is agreement about what happened and why. Importantly, there has been no systematic consideration of how, or if, a particular exclusion could have been prevented. Including children fully as research subjects and participants in exclusions research has been undertaken in a very limited way. The field research reported upon and discussed in Section 2 of this book attempts to remedy some of these gaps in information and debate.

Section 2

The evidence

The evidence: an introduction

The original research evidence was collected at three levels: national, local education authority (LEA) and individual cases of exclusion. National data relate to the 1992–3 academic year and to the autumn term of 1993. The fieldwork was undertaken in three LEAs and individual case studies were carried out during 1994. Detailed information was obtained from 46 LEAs nationally, including a fairly representative range of locations and types of LEA. The case study LEAs include a large county council (LEA 1) and two inner London boroughs (LEAs 2 and 3). Fieldwork in these three LEAs yielded carefully collated data on 265 primary age children excluded from school during the 1993–4 school year. These children are fairly evenly divided between those resident in the county council (134, 50.6 per cent) and those resident in the two inner London boroughs (131, 49.4 per cent).

Individual case studies were conducted for 38 of the 265 children investigated. In all of the in-depth case studies, both home and school-based accounts of the child and their circumstances were analysed. In nearly a third of cases the 'home' account had to be obtained via the social services department. Research in each of the case studies is extensive, involving the analysis of between two and three educational files, as well as three or four in-depth interviews with key actors in relation to an exclusion event (or series of events). Nevertheless it must be remembered in reading the data that there is much that may not have been uncovered in some of the situations investigated. The emphasis in Section 2 is upon the 38 case studies, with the national and LEA data providing a wider context or backdrop to an in-depth analysis of these cases.

Three

National and local authority data

Background

As Section 1 of this book has intimated, school exclusion is an emotive issue, about which it is difficult to gain access to accurate information. In order to try and overcome these difficulties, the research was designed in such a way that at the LEA level of case study, a great deal of effort was put into reassuring individuals about confidentiality as well as involving key individuals in discussions and feedback on data collected. By cross-referencing and checking official records through identifying individual named children excluded over a particular timeframe, accurate data were compiled from official records; these data were of use and interest to the LEAs concerned. When verifying data, it was found that LEA staff could understand better whether information was accurate when it was presented in terms of named children, rather than as summary statistics. LEA staff were thus able to make us aware when excluded primary school children with whom they were working did not appear in the data. There were more difficulties in obtaining good quality national data, therefore these data will only be referred to briefly in this chapter.

The national picture (the 1992–3 school year and autumn term 1993)

National data were obtained from 46 LEAs across England and Wales which replied to a postal questionnaire sent out in January 1994. Contact was made with an additional 17 LEAs which were unable to respond to a questionnaire for a variety of reasons, including not having easily accessible computerized data, pressure of work and staff shortages. The combination of questionnaire, letters and reports, as well as telephone conversations, has enabled a national picture of trends to be obtained.

A comparison of primary and secondary exclusions in the sample revealed that overall primary exclusions represent 14 per cent of all exclusions for 1992–3. Analysis by type of LEA, however, shows that the highest rate of primary school exclusion (18 per cent) is found in London and metropolitan LEAs alike, while county council LEAs show only 11 per cent. During the time the national questionnaire was distributed, indefinite exclusions were still utilized. However, fixed term exclusions were by far the most common type employed by schools, accounting for between two-thirds and four-fifths of recorded exclusions, across the different types of LEA. Metropolitan districts had the highest proportion of primary exclusions in the permanent category and London boroughs had the least.

Characteristics of excluded primary age pupils

LEAs were asked to supply information about the characteristics (age, sex and ethnicity) of excluded primary age pupils. A significant number of LEAs were unable to do this. Thus the data in this subsection are based on the findings from 28 LEAs. The overwhelming majority of excluded primary children were boys, an average proportion of 90 per cent, although this proportion varied a little across the different types of LEAs. It might be expected that a greater proportion of exclusions would be found in the older age range in primary schools, and this was indeed the case in both county councils and metropolitan districts, the majority of respondents. However, this was not the case in London LEAs, where the proportion of exclusions across the primary age range was more evenly divided between the younger and older age categories.

Information obtained on the ethnicity of excluded pupils was the most partial and is arguably one of the most controversial aspects of the exclusion debate. Only 15 of the 46 LEAs responding to the survey were able to supply data by ethnicity: most of these LEAs were either London boroughs or metropolitan districts. Analysis of this relatively restricted sample of LEAs reveals some trends which were borne out in more in-depth case study data. When the proportions of exclusions for four ethnic groups, African-Caribbean, Asian, mixed race/other, and White, were compared with the proportion of these groups in the whole population of the individual LEA (1991 census data), a number of patterns were found. White and Asian pupils tended to be underrepresented, while African-Caribbean and mixed race/other pupils tended to be overrepresented in exclusion statistics by up to three times the proportion in the local population.

Only a minority of LEAs (18) could provide details about reasons why children were excluded from school. The most commonly cited reasons were: refusal to comply with school rules, physical aggression towards other pupils, verbal abuse of teachers and physical aggression towards members of staff. In addition, some LEAs indicated that the recorded reason for exclusion was in reality 'the last straw' in a series of misdemeanours culminating in an exclusion.

Trends and a national estimate

Thirty-four LEAs supplied comments, backed by evidence about trends in primary school exclusion over a four-year period (starting in September 1990). Most LEAs reported an increase in records of primary school exclusions, but in a context of an increase in recorded exclusions overall. Only four LEAs replied indicating that there had been a decrease in primary age exclusions and three LEAs reported that the number of primary school exclusions had 'stayed about the same'. Most LEAs were able to provide data for the whole year 1992–3 in terms of incidence of exclusion but not always by individual child. Therefore the national estimate is based on reported incidences of exclusion. It is estimated that 8,636 children were permanently excluded from both primary and secondary schools in the 1992–3 academic year, a similar figure to that arising from OFSTED reports in the same year (see Table 2.1). There were an estimated 54,423 records of incidences of all types of exclusion in the same year. It is estimated that there were 10,122 incidences of primary exclusions (all types) in this same year, of which 1,215 were likely to be permanent. Autumn 1993 showed an increase in the rate of exclusion, which has since been confirmed by Parsons *et al.* (1995).

Case study LEAs: a profile

One of the London boroughs was one of the few LEAs nationally to report a reduction in primary school exclusions and excluded very few such children permanently. The other London borough had very minimal data on trends and characteristics of excluded primary school children, but had made the interesting decision to contract out its support and EOTAS services to an external provider registered as a charity, 'Cities in Schools'. Both inner London boroughs had substantial Black and minority ethnic sections of the population, which were relatively few in the county council. In many other respects these three LEAs encompass a wide variety of socio-economic, political and educational environments, as this subsection will illustrate. LEA 1 is a shire county in southern England, with over 500 primary schools; it was one of the largest LEAs in England before unitary authorities were established. LEAs 2 and 3 are inner London boroughs with a similar-sized primary school population and number of schools, about 40 of which are primary schools in each borough. Both LEAs 2 and

3 are among the smallest inner London boroughs. At the time of fieldwork these LEAs spanned the political spectrum, with the balance of power being with Liberal Democrats in the county council, with the Labour group in one of the inner London boroughs and with the Conservatives in the other inner London borough.

Overall LEA 1 may seem like a relatively affluent part of England. However, its social geography is one in which a broad range of circumstances are represented. In two of the four divisions in LEA 1 there are areas of inner city deprivation. The other two divisions are often perceived as more affluent but both contain large areas of municipal housing and forces settlements. The size and organization of this LEA made it seem like four different LEAs during the course of fieldwork. There is EBD provision in each area, which was all-age provision (ages 6–16) at the time of fieldwork. EBD provision has since been changed so that there is separate provision for the primary and secondary phases. However, the sheer size of the county, with large expanses of rural areas, means that access to these facilities is very problematic in some areas. Provision has evolved unevenly. There was no behaviour support service at the time of fieldwork, although educational psychologists (EPs) were involved in INSET and GEST projects and were addressing the issue of behaviour support in some localities. The population of this county is overwhelmingly White, with under 2 per cent of the population describing themselves as from Black and minority ethnic groups in the census.

LEA 2 may be typified as an old-style inner London borough which still had a range of support services, such as behaviour support, learning support, psychiatric social work and psychotherapy time attached to the education service. However, these services were reducing as we carried out the fieldwork. This borough has a primary EBD school on the same site as an attendance unit. Socio-economic indicators for the 1991 census show this borough to be at or near the average for inner London boroughs in many respects. An analysis of the ethnic make-up of residents illustrates the multiracial nature of the borough, with Black African, Black Caribbean, and Black 'other' households being the largest groupings of Black and minority ethnic groups.

In contrast, LEA 3 saw itself as one of the new 'lean and mean' or 'hands off' type of LEA, committed to investigating external markets where possible. At the time of fieldwork, off-site units (for children excluded from or not attending school) had been closed to finance a programme of work by Cities in Schools. Part of this programme of work was targeted at primary school children in particular. Cities in Schools was the only provision made for excluded pupils within the borough. The LEA bought places in EBD special schools and other provisions from outside the borough, as and when it was deemed necessary. Census data shows a not dissimilar profile from LEA 2, although a slightly higher proportion of households than in LEA 2 are from Black and minority ethnic groupings in this borough. Again Black Caribbean and Black African households are the most common ethnic

Table 3.1 Number and rate of exclusions (1992–3)

LEA	All exclusions		Primary exclusions only	
	No.	Rate per 1,000	No.	Rate per 1,000
LEA 1	2,560	12.1	352	2.7
LEA 2	568	42.0	101	11.6
LEA 3	606	36.3	37	4.0

groups, but Indian, Asian, Bangladeshi and Chinese households are also present in larger numbers than in LEA 2.

All of the LEAs had both voluntary aided and LEA funded primary schools, with the balance being with LEA schools in LEAs 1 and 2. However, two-thirds of the primary schools in LEA 3 were voluntary aided. Grant maintained schools were only a feature at primary school level in LEA 1, although there were grant maintained schools at secondary level in both LEAs 1 and 2. LEA 3 did not have any such schools in either phase. Voluntary aided status was perceived as a particular problem by LEA education personnel in the London boroughs in relation to obtaining school places for the more problematic youngsters. Voluntary aided schools were described as not always helpful in relation to letting the LEA know whether they had a place to offer a child without first meeting them and their parents and carers – a process which can make informal selection procedures possible. There was also a perception in LEA 3 that such schools did not readily report fixed term exclusions to the LEA.

Case study LEAs: comparing the number and rate of exclusions

In an attempt to present the most meaningful data in this respect, exclusions in each LEA are shown both as numbers and rates per 1,000 school population, with separate figures for primary school pupils only. Table 3.1 shows the records of all types of exclusion for both primary and secondary children in 1992–3. It illustrates that the London boroughs (LEAs 2 and 3) have the highest rate per 1,000 school population. Records of primary school exclusion were much less frequent, but in total still involved some hundreds of children. Fieldwork in each LEA showed a complex picture. The rate of primary school exclusion in LEA 1 was influenced by the fact that a quarter of Year 7 children (12-year-olds) were still in middle schools in 1992–3. These older children accounted for a disproportionate number of primary exclusions in this LEA. LEA 2 had a high rate of recorded exclusion in comparison with the other London borough investigated, but this was largely due to the practice of recording fixed term exclusions. LEA 2 was actually more successful than LEA 3 in avoiding permanent exclusion. The viewpoint that there was an underreporting of fixed term exclusions

Table 3.2 Types of exclusion recorded (by incidence and by individual, shown in brackets below)

	LEA 1[1]		LEA 2		LEA 3		Totals	
Permanent	18	(18)	2	(2)	7	(7)	27	(27)
Indefinite	27	(22)	9	(9)	1	(1)	37	(32)
Aggregate[2]	—		7	(6)	—		7	(6)
Fixed	127	(94)	146	(82)	31	(24)	304	(200)
Total incidences	172		164		39		375	
Total individuals		(134)		(99)		(32)		(265)

1 Figures for LEA 1 relate to one term only. Figures for LEAs 2 and 3 are for the whole year 1993–4.
2 Aggregate exclusion was a term utilized in LEA 2 only, to refer to children who had more than five days exclusion accumulated over a term.

from the large proportion of voluntary aided schools in LEA 3 was put forward a number of times during fieldwork, which may partly explain the relatively low rate of recorded exclusion in this borough.

Analysis of data on file for 265 excluded primary age children

Data available in the education department were collated for primary age children who were identified as having been excluded over a particular timeframe; this related to the autumn term of 1993 only in LEA 1 and the whole school year (1993–4) in LEAs 2 and 3. There were two reasons why whole-year figures were collated in the two London boroughs, but not in the county council. The main reason was that there were insufficient children excluded in one school term in the inner London boroughs to provide a good chance of gaining access to families for the purpose of the in-depth case studies and for a comparison group of a similar size to the children identified in LEA 1. The second reason related to fieldwork practicalities: the collation of reliable data for even one school term in the county council was an onerous task. This stage of the fieldwork in the county council involved the collation of information kept in manual ledgers and filing cabinets to a large extent, and the tracking of files on individual children which sometimes were on the desks of individual caseworkers, across four different divisions of the county. Furthermore, all three sections of the service (admissions/exclusions; special educational needs; educational welfare) were not on the same site in two of the four divisions.

Table 3.2 illustrates how very many fewer individual children are involved in exclusion incidents than might be recorded, if all types of exclusion are noted. Permanent exclusions are of course usually only resorted to once in the relatively short timeframe of a school year – they are very unusual events, although several of our individual case studies of children revealed that they had been the subject of previous permanent exclusion(s) in another school year. Furthermore, some children were the subject of more than one indefinite exclusion even within one school term in LEA 1. However, fixed term exclusions were by far the most common incidences, with some children having several of these over the timeframe monitored. Sometimes a fixed term exclusion was the forerunner to more serious exclusion events.

The number of children who have had more than one exclusion during the period of study make up over a quarter (73, 27.5 per cent) of the children investigated. This is a very small number of primary school children, when one considers that the primary school population in these three LEAs amounted to nearly 150,000 children in the 1993–4 academic year. It would appear that the London boroughs do not resort to several recorded exclusions over a short timeframe as readily as schools do in the county council.

Overall about a quarter of the excluded children were aged between 4 and 8, that is infant school age. About three-quarters of the children were of junior school age, that is between 9 and 11 years of age in the majority, but with some 12-year-old children included in LEA 1, which had middle schools in some areas. As with the national data, about 90 per cent of the 265 cases of exclusion were boys. Only one of the three LEAs had any routine recording of the ethnicity of excluded children; even then the information was not always recorded for a variety of reasons in 20 per cent of the cases investigated. The pattern of exclusion in this LEA very much mirrors the information available from the national questionnaire and from other research with respect to African-Caribbean boys. According to local authority data African-Caribbean children are more numerous in the school population than would be suggested by census data for the whole population. Census data for the 0 to 9-year-old age groups have been used to compare the relative proportions of different Black and minority ethnic children in comparison with the ethnicity of excluded primary age children. In all, over half (41, 52 per cent) of all exclusions in LEA 2 where ethnicity is recorded are of children from Black and minority ethnic groups, whereas they make up less than a third of the primary school population (29.7 per cent). However, the data reveal that it is a very specific ethnic group which is overrepresented among excluded children, namely African-Caribbean children. In this borough the data available show an overrepresentation of African-Caribbean children among excluded primary age pupils to the tune of nearly four times their number in the population. When one considers the fact that the majority of these children are boys (27, 90 per cent), their overrepresentation in the exclusions statistics is really between seven and eight times their number in the school population. In comparison, all other ethnic groups, including Black African and Black 'other' children are underrepresented in exclusion statistics. In fact Asian, Bangladeshi, Chinese, Indian and Pakistani children together make up 6.6 per cent of the primary school population of this LEA, but no recorded cases of exclusion of these children were found during the 1993–4 academic year for LEA 2.

Table 3.3 Reasons for exclusion (given by head teacher)

Reason	% of cases citing this reason			Overall total	
	LEA 1	LEA 2	LEA 3	Nos. cases	% cases
Physical aggression	55	55	57	142	53.6
Verbal abuse	23	11.5	14	46	17.4
Unacceptable behaviour	34	n/a	46	50	18.9
Disobedience	20	10.5	39	43	16.2
Disruption	12	3	18	23	8.7
Other	27	20	12.5	43	16.2
No reason[1]	1.5	—	8	6	2.2

1 No reason was recorded in six cases.

N.b. Figures do not add up to 100 per cent in LEAs 1 and 3 because many cases cited more than one reason for an exclusion. In LEA 2 reasons for exclusion were categorized in a standardized way and therefore do add up to 100 per cent.

Table 3.4 Evidence of high levels of special educational need (i.e. additional support requested from the LEA)

	% of cases where this is a factor			Overall totals	
	LEA 1	LEA 2	LEA 3	Nos. cases	% cases
Statemented	38	15	19	71	26.8
In process of assessment	18	15	13	43	16.2
Total	56	30	32	114	43.0

In LEA 1 and LEA 3 many cases cited more than one reason for incidences of exclusion (see Table 3.3). However, in LEA 2 reasons for exclusion were standardized and coded on a reporting form which schools completed and sent to the LEA when they excluded a child. There is still a remarkable similarity in the main recorded reason for exclusion. Overall physical aggression, usually towards another pupil, was the main recorded reason in over half of primary school exclusions in all three LEAs. Two of the LEAs had records of exclusion which sometimes only had descriptions of behaviour, as 'unacceptable' in some way, although this was not always explained. Verbal abuse comprises a significant proportion of reasons for exclusion, along with disobedient and disruptive behaviour. There were a wide range of 'other' reasons given, including absconding from the school premises, smoking and vandalism.

Evidence of significant special educational need was found in a large proportion of cases in all three LEAs, most dramatically so in LEA 1 (see Table 3.4). It is difficult to offer a precise reason why the differences between the county council and inner London boroughs are so marked, although it

Table 3.5 Evidence of agencies involved with child/family

	% of cases where this was apparent			Overall totals	
	LEA 1	LEA 2	LEA 3	Nos. cases	% cases
Social services	37	33	34	94	35.5
1 + non-mainstream agency[1]	81	89	66	219	82.6

1 Non-mainstream agencies are defined as agencies which only become involved with a child or family if there is an acknowledged need or difficulty, e.g. education welfare departments, social services, child and family guidance clinics and health-based psychiatric interventions.

is likely to relate to policy and practice in the different LEAs with respect to making EBD statements and providing for such pupils. Both the London boroughs had clear policies in their provision for excluded primary age pupils. In all of these LEAs, there was enough concern about many of the children's identified (or possible) special educational needs prior to the exclusion that a formal assessment was taking place and in some cases a statement had been issued. Thus many of the excluded children had already been significantly prioritized within the school to gain access to the limited time of an educational psychologist. Educational psychologist time usually amounted to two half days a school term for most of the primary schools visited and only half a day in the very small schools. However, educational psychologists have very different ways of working in some LEAs which have not been visited in this research and may be more available when schools need them in some localities. Where the children were already statemented at the time of their exclusion, it was almost always for EBD. It was common to initiate or try to initiate a formal assessment process after a child was excluded from school.

For the 65 children across the three LEAs who had more serious (permanent, indefinite, aggregate) types of exclusion during the 1993–4 academic year, evidence of special educational need was even more apparent. If other documented indicators of the need for additional support are included, such as the use of a behaviour support team with the individual and educational psychology advice and observation, 85 per cent of these children had evidence of either special educational need or strong evidence of concern that this might be an issue.

According to information available on education files, the majority of children and families were already in receipt of support from non-mainstream agencies (see Table 3.5). Non-mainstream agencies have been defined as those agencies which only become involved with a child or family when problems have arisen, at home or school (or in both contexts). Social services was the most frequent type of support families were receiving. Other agencies included educational welfare/education social work, child and family guidance/therapy, hospital-based interventions and occasionally charities (such as the NSPCC). It is likely that this part of the research has under-estimated the range of support families have received, as the research relies upon the information supplied to and recorded in education departments. Education departments only had this kind of information about families if the child had education welfare involvement or a statement or was in the process of formal assessment for special educational needs. Nevertheless these data suggest a group of children and families already well known to be in need by a range of services.

Again for the 65 children who had the more serious types of exclusion there was strong evidence of major concerns about and within the families and home circumstances. Over three-quarters (76.6 per cent) of these children had either social services involvement with the family, child and family guidance or psychiatric services, or some other form of therapeutic and family-based work. There was evidence of the involvement of one or more non-mainstream agencies in the vast majority of cases (61, 91 per cent). There was a total absence of any data in the special needs and educational welfare sections of the education service on only four of the children who had serious exclusions. This may be explained by the findings in individual case studies, described in the next chapter. Individual case studies showed that many of the children had very disrupted backgrounds, particularly those children who had been in the care of the local authority. Children who moved between different parts of the county in LEA 1 , across London boroughs and to and from other parts of the country, sometimes did not get their educational records transferred quickly enough for appropriate provision to be in place. There was also evidence in the fieldwork that schools were not always told about the level of a child's need because of a belief that a school would not accept the child if they knew.

Analysis of the information across schools in each LEA produced some interesting and thought-provoking results. At the level of LEA, a higher proportion of primary schools had excluded a child during the autumn term of 1993 in the London boroughs (LEA 2 1 : 3; LEA 3 1 : 5) in comparison with the county council (LEA 1 1 : 8). However, the majority of schools had officially excluded only one or two children and usually for a fixed term period. Many of these exclusions were under five days in duration and do not legally have to be reported to the LEA, although all the LEAs encouraged schools to report such exclusions. These reported exclusions were disproportionately from county rather than voluntary aided/controlled schools in each LEA.

The research indicates that some schools are certainly more successful than others in avoiding a recorded fixed term exclusion for a primary age child. The permanent exclusions appear to be a much more haphazard, less predictable and rare event (i.e. in terms of occurrence at a particular school). However, there is still a recording issue here. Some head teachers reported a particularly good relationship with the LEA, usually because they had been part of various LEA behaviour management initiatives; such schools expected the LEA to take them seriously when they said they could not continue to contain a child. According to some head teachers, such a child was likely to go on to a special school or unit and not necessarily have a record of a permanent exclusion.

Each LEA had schools which stood out as relatively high excluders, in that they had excluded several children in a relatively short period of time. For example six (out of a total of over 500) primary schools in LEA 1 had excluded five or more children in a one-term period. Eight out of a total of 37 schools in LEA 2 had excluded five or more children by the end of a whole school year. Yet only two out of a total of 41 schools in LEA 3 had excluded five or more children over the same time period. Thus the relatively high-excluding schools at primary level are those which used and recorded fixed term exclusions. Fieldwork tended to show that this related to some extent to the head teachers' view of fixed term exclusion as a disciplinary measure. Fieldwork in LEAs 1 and 2 also revealed particular situations in relation to an EBD special school in each of the LEAs. In both LEAs these special schools had fairly major staffing problems, relating to sickness in one case and both staff recruitment and sickness in the other case. Also there was no possibility of such schools being able to set in motion speedy arrangements to transfer children to other facilities, as this usually would mean the extremely expensive option of an out-of-County residential placement.

Evidence from the case studies of exclusion, as well as interviews with LEA staff, would suggest that extreme caution would be needed before any assessment of patterns of exclusion across primary schools is made. One reason for this is the belief, expressed most strongly in LEA 3, that voluntary aided/controlled schools did not always report fixed term exclusions to the LEA. As has already been stated, most of the exclusions were under five days in duration and schools do not have to report them to the LEA anyway. Possibly some county schools also do not always report these exclusions. Another reason is the evidence that information is not always accurately recorded at LEA level. For example one primary school, which was spoken of highly by a senior member of staff in LEA 2 because it was said not to resort to exclusion, was found during fieldwork to be the *highest* fixed term excluder in the borough. Much longer-term monitoring, over a period of years, would be needed to make a fair assessment about any patterns of exclusion across primary schools.

Summary and conclusions

The national questionnaire illustrated that data collection systems about exclusion from school are in many ways inadequate. Most importantly there is a failure in many local authorities to distinguish between incidence of exclusion and individual child excluded. There is a failure systematically to collect data about all of the key characteristics of excluded pupils – even basic characteristics like age and sex of individuals were absent in some

LEA data. There is insufficient LEA monitoring of exclusions by ethnicity, which is particularly worrying given the evidence presented here (and found by other research referred to in Chapter 2) that certain groups, particularly African-Caribbean boys are overrepresented in exclusions statistics. There is also a lack of systematic monitoring of whether excluded children have evidence of special educational needs. However, the fieldwork in the three LEAs illustrated why this is so, practically if not politically. The main reasons were lack of staff, sometimes through absence and ill health and occasionally because an appointment had not been made. There were also staff changes in all three case study LEAs during the period of fieldwork, which meant that different people had the responsibility for channelling, recording and reporting upon the data. Furthermore, as already stated, schools did not always supply the LEA with all the information requested and there were very limited possibilities for following up and getting such data, again because of lack of staff. Both of the London boroughs had only one member of staff to deal with recording and following up exclusions; in each case this was only supposed to be a relatively small part of their work. Both individuals reported that it tended to dominate their working week. A similar picture was found in the county council, where each division had only one person dealing with exclusions, for part of their working week.

The broad patterns of exclusion are in many ways more predictable, with urban and inner-city environments having higher rates of reported exclusion. But a greater unevenness between schools was detectable within case study LEAs. However, if primary schools excluded at all during the 1993–4 academic year it was usually only one or more fixed term exclusions. It is noticeable that there were proportionately fewer reported exclusions from voluntary aided and controlled schools than would be expected from their proportion of school provision. Exclusion from primary school is shown to be a relatively rare event, with permanent primary school exclusions being even more unusual. It is very much an event which is happening predominantly to young boys: when primary age girls are excluded from school they appear to be children in the most extreme circumstances. It is clear that the very rarity of the event itself suggests that more practical attention should be given to the educational and social needs of these children. There is certainly evidence that many of these young children have acknowledged special educational needs and have come to the attention of non-mainstream agencies, usually because of concern about their family circumstances. These latter generalizations are all the more true for the small group of children who have had the more serious types of exclusion (variously referred to as indefinite, aggregate, and of course, permanent). The in-depth individual case studies reported upon in the next few chapters in this section will further illuminate the circumstances surrounding these children's exclusions.

Four

The case studies of excluded children

Background

This chapter will present the characteristics of the 38 children who form the basis for the individual case studies. The case study children were excluded from schools in two of the three LEAs referred to in the last chapter. One LEA is a County Council, the other is an inner London Borough. It will outline their exclusion(s), their home circumstances and possible sources of difficulty or stress in their lives. The children will be identified by a fictional first name throughout the chapter and thereafter when individual children are referred to. The information presented is intended to be a background to the chapters which follow it and report separately on home and school accounts of events surrounding a child's exclusion(s) from school. The child's view is included in the 'home' chapter. The characteristics and circumstances of individual children are illustrated in Tables 4.1 and 4.2. The summary characteristics and circumstances of the whole group of case studies are illustrated in Tables 4.3 to 4.9.

Characteristics and circumstances of individual children

Although much of this chapter deals with summary information for the whole group of children, information will first be presented about the children as individuals. Information will be presented in this way in order to illustrate both the range of circumstances and commonalities found in this group of children. The tables may also serve as a reference point when comments are made about individual children. These tables attempt to portray the complexity of the circumstances investigated. Table 4.1 illustrates the characteristics, circumstances, schooling and exclusions experienced by the children. Table 4.2 portrays life events which are likely to be experienced as stressful for the children, particularly when they are experienced concurrently or over a short period of time. The idea behind presenting data in this way derives from the work of Chandler (1981) in his 'Source of stress inventory', which identifies 37 possible life events which may be a cause of stress in children. We have concentrated upon 11 relatively severe events with an additional catch-all 'other' category. Table 4.2 illustrates evidence of a range of between one and 11 serious stresses in the lives of the children investigated. The mean number of stresses per child was 6.7. The child with evidence of only one major stress in his background had lost his father – there was some evidence that this may have been due to suicide. The circumstances and issues identified in these tables will be explored in more depth later in the chapter.

Basic characteristics of the sample of excluded children

The age, sex and ethnicity of the whole sample will be presented in this subsection.

Table 4.3 shows that the children ranged in age from 6 (Year 2) to 12 (Year 7). This was broadly representative of the data on file in the case-study LEAs overall, as exclusions in the reception year and Year 1 were very rare. The proportions of children in these broad age bands almost exactly replicates that found in county councils in the national data, but there are fewer children in the younger age group in the London borough than is true for these types of LEA in the national data.

Table 4.4 shows that the great majority of case studies (87 per cent) were boys, which is almost in keeping with national data and the data collated at LEA level. The small number (5, 13 per cent) of girls in the study is actually an overrepresentation in comparison with their proportion in the national and LEA data; it is essential, though, in the researchers' view, to represent this minority appropriately.

The girls ranged in age from 9 to 12 years (Years 4–7) and all were White. All five of these cases were of children from extremely difficult and disrupted home circumstances. All of the girls had spent time in the care of the local authority, with four of them being resident in children's homes at the time of fieldwork. Among the indicators of difficulty and stress for these young girls were allegations of sexual abuse of the girls in two cases; the mother of a third girl was in prison during her early childhood and there was evidence of emotional abuse by the grandparents who had taken over her care. In the other two cases there was evidence of neglect and emotional abuse. Four of the five girls had a permanent exclusion during the period of investigation, while the fifth girl had been attending school intermittently before her exclusion and part-time afterwards. Two of the

Table 4.1 The children – key characteristics, where resident, types of exclusion (1993–4), reasons, schooling

Child	(1) Sex	(2) Year group	(3) Ethnicity	(4) Where resident	(5) Types of exclusion 1993–4	(6) School attended at time	(7) New to school in 1993–4	(8) Main reasons for exclusion	(9) Transfer to spec. sch. post-excl.
Adam	m	5	B(o)	m → fp → m	**F**(×2)	m		P(A&C)	
Alan	m	2	W	m → fp → ch	**F**	m	y	P(A)	
Andrew	m	6	W	fp → ↑ ch	F → P	m		HLD, A, P(C)	y
Andy	m	4	W	m → ↑ f	**P**, I → P	m	y	HLD	
Bob	m	5	B(C)	m ↔ f?	**F**	m	y	D, P(A&C)	
Bradley	m	2	W	m & sf	**F**, PT, P	m	y	HLD	y
Catherine	f	7	W	fp	**P**	ss		HLD, P(A&C), A, O	n/a
Charlie	m	4	W	m & sf → fp	**F**	m		O	
Chris	m	3	W	m	**F** → P	m	y	HLD	y
Dale	m	5	M	m	**F**	m	y	P(C)	
Daniel	m	7	W	m & sf	**F**(×2)	m		P(C)	
Gareth	m	5	W	m & f	**F**, P	m		HLD, A	p
Gerald	m	5	W	m → ↑ f	**F**, P	m	y	HLD, P(C)	y
Henry	m	4	W	m ↔ ↑ f	F, **I** → R	m	y	HLD, P(C), A, O	
Ian	m	7	W	m & f	**I**, PT	m		D, P(C)	
Jeremiah	m	4	M	m ↔ f ↔ fp	I → P	m	y	HLD, A	
Jerry	m	3	W	m & sf	L, **F**, I → R	m		HLD, P(A&C)	p
Joanna	f	5	W	m & sf → ch	**F**	m		HLD, P(C), A	
Joe	m	6	W	ch → fp	F, **I** → P	m		HLD	
Jordon	m	3	B(A)	m	**F**	m		P(C)	
Katy	f	4	W	gp → m	**F**, P	m	y	HLD	
Kevin	m	7	W	f & sm	**F**(×2), P	m	y	HLD	
Levi	m	2	B(A)	m & sf	**F**(×3)	m		P(A&C)	
Lewis	m	3	W	m & sf	L, **F**(×2), I → R	m		HLD, A, O	p
Manus	m	2	B(C)	m	F(×2), **I** → P	m	y	P(A&C), O	y
Nathan	m	7	W	m & sf	F(×2), **I** → P	m	y	HLD, A, O	y
Paul	m	7	W	f & sm ↔ m	**P**	m		P(A)	
Peter	m	6	W	m & f	**F**(×2)	su		HLD	
Pippa	f	5	W	m → fp → ch	**P**	m		HLD, P(C), A	
Rajah	m	6	M	m	**I** → P	m	y	HLD, P(A&C)	y

	(1) sex	(2)	(3) ethnicity	(4) where resident	(5) types of exclusion	(6) school	(7) new	(8)	(9)
Sarah	f	7	W	ch	F(×2), PT	m	y	HLD, P(A&C)	
Shamus	m	4	W	m & sf	F(×2)	m		D, P(C)	
Shane	m	6	W	m & sf	I → P	m		HLD, P(C), O	
Steve	m	3	W	ch	F	m	y	P(C), A	
Thomas	m	6	W	m & f	F, P	m	y	HLD	
Tommy	m	6	W	ch	F, I, **P**	ss		P(A&C)	n/a
Tony	m	5	W	m & sf	**F**	ss		P(C), A	
Wayne	m	4	W	fp → ch	**F**, P	m	y	HLD, A, O	p

Key

Column (1) sex	m = male f = female
Column (3) ethnicity	B(A) = Black African B(C) = Black Caribbean B(o) = Black other M = mixed race W = white
Column (4) where child resident	f = father m = mother sf = stepfather sm = stepmother ch = children's home fp = foster parents ↔ = movement between parents ? = unclear
Column (5) types of exclusion	L = lunchtime F = fixed term I = indefinite P = permanent PT = part-time attendance I → R reinstated I → P indefinite went to permanent Exclusion highlighted in bold is the one investigated
Column (6) school attended at the time	m = mainstream su = special unit ss = special school
Column (7) New to school in 1993–4	y = yes
Column (8)	A = absconding D = disruption HLD = high level disruption P(A) = physical aggression to adults P(C) = physical aggression to children O = other
Column (9)	y = yes p = planned n/a = not applicable (already in special education)

Table 4.2 The children – indicators of stress

Child	(1) Family breakdown	(2) Time in care (c) Social work involvement	(3) Multiple moves Disruption	(4) Disability Bereavement	(5) Violence Abuse	(6) Major accident/ incident	(7) Police/ courts involvement	(8) Substance misuse	(9) SEN statement FA assess in class	(10) Ever had serious excl.	(11) No member of household in paid work	(12) Other	Total
Adam	•								•(IC)				2
Alan	•	•(c)	•		•	•	•		•(S)	•(P)	•	•	11
Andrew	•	•(c)	•	•	•			•	•(S)	•(P)	•	•	7
Andy	•	•	•		•	•		•	•(S)	•(Px2)			10
Bob	•	•		•		•			•(S)				7
Bradley	•	•(c)	•	•	•	•		•	•(S)	•(P)		•	6
Catherine	•	•(c)	•		•	•			•(S)	•(P)			11
Charlie	•	•(c)	•		•	•	•		•(IC)				8
Chris	•	•	•				•	•	•(S)	•(P)		•	9
Dale				•				•	•(IC)			•	5
Daniel													1
Gareth	•		•		•				•(FA)	•(P)			4
Cerald	•		•		•				•(S)	•(P)		•	5
Ilenry			•			•			•(S)	•(P)	•	•	6
Ian			•		•	•	•	•	•(FA)	•(I)(PT)			5
Jeremiah	•	•(c)			•					•(P)		•	8
Jerry	•	•(c)							•(S)	•(I)		•	4
Joanna	•	•(c)	•		•				•(FA)				6
Joe	•	•	•	•	•			•	•(FA)	•(P)			7
Jordon			•									•	5
Katy	•	•(c)	•	•	•		•		•(FA)	•(P)			8
Kevin	•	•(c)	•	•	•	•	•		•(FA)	•(P)			11

Name	(1)	(2)	(3)	(4)	(5)	(6)	(7)	(8)	(9) SEN	(10)	(11)	(12)	average
Levi	•								• (FA)			•	3
Lewis	•	• (c)	•						• (S)	• (I)		•	4
Manus	•	• (c)	•						• (S)	• (P)	•	•	11
Nathan	•	•							• (S)	• (P)		•	5
Paul	•	•	•						• (S)	• (P)	•	•	8
Peter	•		•				•		• (S)	• (P)	•	•	5
Pippa	•	• (c)	•				•		• (S)	• (P)	•	•	10
Rajah	•	•	•				•		• (FA)	• (P)	•	•	9
Sarah	•	• (c)	•				•		• (IC)	• (PT)	•		9
Shamus	•	• (c)	•					•	• (IC)		•		8
Shane	•	•							• (FA)	• (P)		•	6
Steve	•	• (c)	•			•	•	•	• (IC)		•		9
Thomas	•					•							3
Tommy	•	• (c)	•						• (S)	• (P)	•	•	8
Tony	•		•						• (S)	• (P)	•	•	5
Wayne	•	• (c)	•						• (S)	• (P)	•		7
Total	33	25	23	23	11	11	15	9	33	28	23	22	6.7 average

Key

• indicates that this potential source of stress is present

Column (2)   time in care indicated by (c)

Column (9) SEN   S = statemented
FA = in process of formal assessment
IC = in-class support

Column (10)   serious exclusion defined as the following:
P = permanent
I = indefinite
PT = part-time schooling

Table 4.3   Year group in school

Year group	Nos. (%)
R/1	—
2	4
3	5
Subtotal (Years R/1–3)	9 (23.7)
4	7
5	8
6	7
7	7
Subtotal (Years 4–7)	29 (76.3)
Total	38 (100)

Table 4.4   Sex of children

Sex	Nos. (%)
Boys	33 (87)
Girls	5 (13)
Total	38 (100)

Table 4.5   Ethnicity of children

Ethnic group	Nos. (%)
Black African	2
Black Caribbean	2
Black other	1
Subtotal Black (A, C, o)	5 (13)
Mixed race	3 (8)
White	30 (79)
Total	38 (100)

girls were statemented (EBD) and a third girl was in the process of formal assessment.

Table 4.5 shows that over three-quarters (79 per cent) of the children came from White families. Black (African, Caribbean and other) families formed a significant grouping (13 per cent), with children of mixed race being another important category in this research (8 per cent). The majority of these families were found in the inner London borough. As the last chapter has shown, the ethnicity of excluded children is often not recorded, although where data are available there tends to be an overrepresentation of

Table 4.6 Evidence of special educational need
(at the time of interview)

Level of need	Nos. (%)
Statemented	18 (47.4)
In process of FA	10 (26.3)
Seen EP	3 (7.9)
In school support	2 (5.3)
Unclear	1 (2.6)
None	4 (10.5)
Total	38 (100)

Black and mixed-race children. It would appear then that the ethnic groups who came to our attention in the case study part of the research are broadly representative of trends illustrated in the national data.

Evidence of special educational need (SEN)

Identifying the likelihood or assessed level of special educational need in these children was in some ways like following a moving target. The majority of children with special educational needs are catered for within the schools' resources. The LEA only become involved if the school, backed by the educational psychologist, decided that the child should go forward for formal assessment and possible statementing. The new Code of Practice, which came into force after the exclusions investigated, clearly outlines the preceding stages which are the responsibility of the school and support agencies. Table 4.6 outlines the children's SEN status at the time of interview, which was usually about six months or less after the event(s) under investigation. The situation at the point of exclusion is also explained.

Table 4.6 shows that the great majority (33, 87 per cent) of children had some clear evidence of special educational need, with nearly half (18, 47.4 per cent) of the sample holding a statement for special educational need at the time of interview. In some cases schools had attempted to start the formal assessment process prior to the exclusion but had been refused. In other cases there was some uncertainty about whether a child had been statemented in another part of the country or even within the LEA. Thus schools were not slow in identifying these children, but the system was cumbersome and slow in addressing their needs. There were no available national data on the SEN status of excluded primary school children with which to make comparison, although information at LEA level suggested that special educational needs were likely to be associated with a large proportion of excluded primary age children (e.g. in LEA 1 38 per cent, in LEA 2 15 per cent of children were statemented at the time of their exclusion). However, data at this level included only statemented children and those in the process of formal assessment (LEA 1 18 per cent, LEA 2 15 per cent), thus the other levels of in-school support would not be recorded on case files in the LEA.

Statemented children form a significant group among the case-study children; over a third (13, 34 per cent) of pupils were statemented at the time of their exclusion and nearly half (18, 47.3 per cent) by the time they were interviewed a few months later. EBD (14) or EBD/MLD (3) was the reason for the statement in all but one case, where the child had a statement for a learning difficulty. However, in this case the child underwent a reassessment after his permanent exclusion from a mainstream primary school and was moved to an EBD special unit. There is an overrepresentation of statemented children in the case studies in comparison with the overall sampling frame, which would indicate that under a third of the children in LEAs 1 and 2 combined (66, 28.3 per cent) had a statement at the time of their exclusion.

Most children who were in the process of formal assessment at the time of interview were not at this stage at the time of their exclusion. Formal assessment started after the child had been excluded from school in eight out of the ten cases recorded this way in Table 4.6. In seven of these eight cases there were circumstances which helped to explain the fact that there was no record of a formal assessment for special educational needs prior to the exclusion taking place. In over half (5) of these cases the child was new to the school. In one case the school had requested formal assessment of a child and had been refused, in another case the school had been without a permanent head teacher for some time and normal systems within the school were under strain. In one of the two cases where it appeared that the school viewed the child as simply naughty, rather than as having a special educational need, a formal assessment started after his permanent exclusion from school.

In five of the six cases where there was no evidence of the child being in the process of formal assessment but being in receipt of in-class support for special educational needs, there was major social services involvement in the family and a great deal of disruption in the child's schooling. All of these five children had spent time in the care of the local authority during the year in which the exclusion under investigation took place.

In the case of Dale, for example, there was no evidence of current social services involvement with the family but there was evidence of special educational need, sufficient to require in-class support, but insufficient to require formal assessment and statementing. His behaviour could be volatile, according to both home and school accounts. Practically his behaviour did provide something of a challenge to a class teacher of 28 children, 12 of whom had some level of identified special educational need, with three of these children holding statements. However, his class teacher emphasized the positive aspects of the child and both she and the head teacher were in agreement about the need for his fixed term exclusion, as a disciplinary measure.

Table 4.7 Type of exclusion investigated

Type of exclusion	Nos. (%)
Permanent	6 (15.8)
Indefinite	8 (21.0)
Fixed	24 (63.2)
Total	38 (100)

There was no evidence of documented special educational need in five cases. In two of these cases it appeared that the school regarded the child as 'naughty' rather than in need of special educational support. In two further cases the child was new to the school, and in the fifth case the parent had refused help from outside agencies. In this last case the parent was a psychotherapist and was of the opinion that she could help the child herself. In one of the more extreme cases (Jeremiah) where the child was new to the school, he had in fact attended seven or eight different schools by the age of 10, had spent time living in a women's refuge and also in bed and breakfast accommodation. At the age of 9 Jeremiah and his family were asked to leave a women's refuge because of his behaviour; later in the same year he stabbed his older brother with a kitchen knife and tried to do the same to his younger brother. His mother had already requested that social services accommodate him. Foster placements broke down because of his behaviour and his last social worker had tried to obtain a place for him at a residential therapeutic environment. This had not been possible to achieve by the time of interview. In fact he had been sent home to live with his mother again, because no suitable placement could be obtained for him.

Exclusions: types and reasons

It was decided from the outset not just to follow through the most serious types of recorded exclusion, in order to investigate whether the different types of exclusion had a different function within the education system. Thus the great majority of children in the case studies appeared initially (that is before files were cross-referenced and interviews conducted) to have only had a relatively minor exclusion.

As Table 4.7 shows, it was found that although at the start of the investigation nearly two-thirds (24, 63.2 per cent) of the children had only been the subject of a fixed term exclusion within the timescale of the sampling frame, they had very often had previous exclusions. In over three-quarters (29, 76 per cent) of all exclusion cases investigated there was clear evidence of previous exclusions from school and many of the children also had subsequent exclusions by the time they were interviewed. Table 4.2 shows that in nearly two-thirds (23, 61 per cent) of the cases, the child had a

Table 4.8   Reasons for exclusion

Reason	Nos. cases citing reason (%)
Physical aggression (C only)	13 (34)
Physical aggression (A&C)	11 (29)
High level disruption	23 (53)
Disruption	3 (8)
Absconding	12 (32)
Other	8 (21)

Numbers do not add up to 38 cases, as many children had more than one reason for their exclusion.
A = adults, C = children

permanent exclusion at some time, including the permanent exclusion under investigation. In addition four (11 per cent) children had indefinite exclusions and in effect had been part-time attenders at school for considerable periods. The great majority of children had other exclusions within six months of the one(s) followed up. In only one case of fixed term exclusion was there no evidence of previous exclusions and no subsequent exclusion within six months of the exclusion investigated. Table 4.1 summarizes the type and number of exclusions the children had during the 1993–4 school year. The type of exclusion originally investigated and featuring in Table 4.2 is emphasized. By the end of the 1993–4 academic year nearly half (18, 47 per cent) of the original 38 children had a permanent exclusion and in addition another two children were only part-time attenders at school. This high incidence of serious types of exclusion is partly explained by the fact that five of the indefinite exclusions went to permanent status and only three indefinitely excluded children were reinstated in their original school during this time. In some (7) other instances a fixed term exclusion was a forerunner to a more serious type of exclusion later in the school year.

Teachers often cited more than one reason for an exclusion at interview, although data at the local authority may only record one reason or a general description, such as 'unacceptable' or 'uncontrollable' behaviour. In several incidences we found that schools played down some of the events, particularly where they were of a very violent, sexual or dangerous nature. All of the reasons, in Table 4.8, relate to the reasons schools gave for excluding a child. Physical aggression to children or both adults and children was one of the behaviours most frequently connected to the exclusion of children in the case studies. This is a higher proportion (63 per cent) than is found in data at LEA level (55 per cent of cases in each LEA) and is much more of an issue in these cases than the national data would suggest. This may be explained in part by the fact, already mentioned, that the full range of incidents was not always reported to the local authority or even itemized in letters to parents and carers. It may also be explained by the slight over-representation of children with special educational needs and more severe types of exclusion in the sample. Table 4.8 shows that many individual children displayed a range of behaviours, of which physical aggression is often a part. Table 4.8 focuses only on the three main behaviours cited by schools as reasons for an individual's exclusion(s).

The disruption caused by these children has been defined as 'high level' in most cases, in that it has affected more than the children and teacher in the individual's class. That is, the individual's behaviour has tended to have an impact on the running of the whole school, particularly the role of the head teacher. Such children often spent considerable periods of time talking through particular events with their head teacher and sometimes working in their office. Many of the children had major outbursts and tantrums outside the classroom, often at lunch and break times, and as Table 4.8 indicates, absconding was cited as a reason for exclusion in a substantial group of children. Interviews with head teachers revealed that an even larger group of the children (17, 48 per cent) had absconded at some time during their period at the school. In most cases absconding involved the child running away from the school site altogether. In several cases (5), head teachers said they felt they had to use physical restraint on a child, to protect the child from themselves and sometimes to protect others. None of these teachers had any formal training about how to use restraint or holding techniques.

There was a wide range of 'other' reasons given for exclusion, including bullying, sexist and racist abuse, reasons which might in some cases be more properly included in the category of physical aggression. Damage to school property was a relatively minor issue, but destruction of other children's work and property was fairly common.

Home circumstances

Table 4.2 summarizes the main evidence in relation to the possible sources of stress in the children's home circumstances and background. Exclusion from school and special educational need are in themselves recognized as indicators, as well as sources of stress for a child (Chandler, 1985). We have already seen that multiple exclusions from school are common for this group of children and that special educational need is also a significant factor. In addition these children had to cope with a wide range of other stresses, which will now be presented and illustrated.

Family breakdown was the most common link in the background of these children: only 4 (11 per cent) of the children lived with both original birth parents (see Table 4.9). One child's father had died – the head teacher was of the opinion that the death could have been a suicide. Family circumstance is defined in relation to the children under investigation and with whom they were resident at the time of interview. However, it must be recognized that household composition and place of residence was a rather fluid concept in many of the cases, sometimes because the children were

Table 4.9   Where child resident at time of fieldwork

Parents/carers	Nos. (%)
Two-parent households	
both birth parents	4
one birth parent/one step	9
Subtotal	13 (34.25)
Single-parent households	
mother	11
father	2
Subtotal	13 (34.25)
In care of local authority (SSD)	
children's home	8
foster parents	3
Subtotal	11 (29)
Unclear	1 (2.5)
Total	38 (100)

being 'looked after' by the local authority (29 per cent) and would be re-turned home when possible, or because children moved residence between parents. It was rare for children to have both birth parents living with them in the same household: single-parent households (34 per cent) and house-holds including a step-parent (24 per cent) were more common. The fluidity of the situation in some households is illustrated in one case where we were unable to establish which of the parents lived in the house with one young boy, who shared the house with two older sisters. In this household we ceased further enquiries when we were alerted by the head teacher that social services were about to become reinvolved with the family, because of information they had been given suggesting that there was not always an adult staying in the house overnight. In two other cases, the parent who replied indicating that they would be willing to see us was not the parent living with the child by the time we came to visit, a matter of weeks later. In some cases parents were very well aware that relationship breakdown was a contributory factor in explaining their child's behaviour. The major-ity of children living at home lived in rented accommodation, which was in most cases owned by the local authority or by a housing association. Only four children lived in owner-occupied property.

Nearly two-thirds (61 per cent) of households had no form of paid employment. Those families where there was an adult in employment were very varied. A minority of households could be described as in professional employment (3). In two of these households both parents were in full-time employment and could be described as relatively affluent. In the third house-hold, the individual was a single parent and had the support of an au pair with her son. The parent in a fourth household also had professional quali-fications but was not in paid employment. In other households (5) where there was full-time employment, all had the father or stepfather in paid work. Types of employment included office and factory work, a small business and the Navy. Several households (4) also reported that their paid employment was casual, and two women worked part-time during school hours. Lack of paid employment may of course not always be experienced as a stressful experience, but it is associated with economic hardship, which is likely to bring its own form of stress.

Nearly half the children had spent time in the care of the local authority (17, 44.7 per cent) during the school year in which they experienced an exclusion, although this was again usually a rather fluid situation, with six of these children living with their parents at the time of the exclusion. In addition another eight families had recent or current social work involvement. Thus in total two-thirds (25, 66 per cent) of the families had some significant involvement with social services departments.

Linked in part to both family breakdown, as well as social services involvement with families, was evidence of numerous moves in residence and often schools too. Disruption of this sort was in evidence in half the families (19, 50 per cent). Several (4) of these families had spent time living in bed and breakfast accommodation. In some of the more extreme cases children had been in so many schools in different parts of the country that the child's social worker was unsure whether or not they had been through formal assessment or had been statemented for special educational needs in another part of the country. For example, by the age of 10 Jeremiah had attended seven or eight different schools. On the other hand there were other children who had multiple moves between parents, foster parents and children's homes and yet had been statemented. In the cases of two brothers (Wayne and Andrew), aged 8 and 11, who were statemented for EBD, they had lived at 34 different addresses at the time of interview. These children went to the same mainstream school, yet arrived in separate social services taxis because their relationship with each other was so negative. The children's home where they were resident was not accepting any other young children while they were resident there.

In well over half (23, 60.5 per cent) of the families there was evidence of violence and abuse in various forms, both between adults and between adults and children. The most common type of abuse was emotional, coupled with general neglect; this type of abuse was in evidence in all of this subgroup of 23 children. There was clear evidence of physical violence in a number of cases (5), towards the mother in all of these cases and sometimes the child as well. There were allegations of sexual abuse in five cases. In two cases the children were violent towards their parent: in one case a 10-year-old boy (Shane) had witnessed his father hitting his mother and was also hit himself; he started to hit his mother after his father left. In the other case, Pippa, herself the subject of emotional abuse as well as neglect, started to hit her disabled mother. Pippa's behaviour led her mother to request she be taken into temporary care. She made frequent attempts to go back to her mother when she absconded from school.

Another issue mentioned was drinking and occasionally other substance misuse of one or both parents (10, 26 per cent). In two cases it was the children who were involved in the substance misuse. In the case of Kevin, he had stolen some miniature whiskies with his friend and had become drunk in a public place. In the second case Nathan had become involved with teenagers and had engaged in glue sniffing. Often information supplied about substance misuse in adults was associated with a range of other issues. Alan's social services file records alcohol misuse by his mother, physical violence from his father and concern about pornographic material in the home. Alan was excluded from school for physical aggression directed towards adults.

The police or courts had been involved with over a third (15, 39 per cent) of the children's families, for incidents other than child protection and domestic violence. Reasons were very varied, ranging from parents imprisoned, charges involving assault and drunk and disorderly behaviour and arson. In two cases police were involved in response to attacks on the family. In one case a family was firebombed in connection to the belief circulating in the local neighbourhood that the house was a centre for the circulation of (allegedly) pornographic material. In another case a mixed-race family had been subjected to both racial harassment and nuisance calls and threats to the child's mother. The racial harassment in the latter case had resulted in the family being rehoused by the local authority, whence the nuisance calls and threats to the mother started.

In eight families the children were directly involved in incidents which had involved the police; in three cases these incidents could be described as relating to anti-social activities, vandalism in two cases. In one case, Andy created a motorbike accident by jumping into the road brandishing a knife. In the other five cases the police were involved because of the need for appropriate care and protection of the child. In two instances the police were called by the parents because the child had absconded. Two children were the victims of cruel, even life-threatening behaviour (in one case) from their peers in the locality of their home.

In another particularly dramatic case, Charlie's foster parents were so alarmed by his behaviour that they called the police, who took him to hospital where he had to be physically restrained in order to stop him hurting himself (one of this child's foster parents was a practising teacher of children with EBD). In only one case (Ian) was any association made between the child's exclusion from school and the incident involving the police. This was in one of the cases of vandalism which occurred during a period when the child attended school only part-time.

There was a wide range of additional sources of stress in most families. Major incidents or accidents were in evidence in nearly a third (12, 32 per cent) of households. Such incidents ranged from the more extreme events, such as a family home which was firebombed (referred to above), a child (Catherine) setting a fire which resulted in the death of her baby brother, to relatively minor road accidents. In addition there were other indications of problems and difficulties in some households, such as children truanting from school (3) and parents with disabilities (6). Two families cited racial abuse and harassment as a source of stress to the family; one such family is referred to above.

Three of the four parents with professional backgrounds were sufficiently concerned about their child that they paid for private consultations in the hope of gaining some insight to their child's behaviour; in two cases the child was seen by a psychologist; in the other case a private psychiatrist undertook four sessions with the boy. There was a tendency in these fam-ilies to want an individual-based explanation for their child's behaviour. Two of the families had actively rejected family-based support and a third family were divided on the issue, with the father refusing to go to any further sessions after attending one session at a child and family guidance clinic. In the fourth household a great deal of emphasis was placed on the child's special educational needs (he was statemented after his permanent exclusion from school), but his mother was also willing to consider the possible impact of the divorce between herself and his father, as well as his relationship with his stepfather.

Summary and conclusions

This chapter has attempted to produce a background to the accounts given by parents/carers, children and teachers, about the circumstances surround-ing and factors pertinent to a child's exclusion(s) from school. The inten-tion is to remind the reader that the child who is behaving in a way which results in an exclusion from primary school may in part at least have their behaviour explained by reference to these circumstances and stresses. The point is being made that exclusion from school is an additional source of stress and disadvantage for children who already have a great deal to cope with in their lives. It can be argued that many (even the majority?) of these children should be viewed as 'needy' rather than 'naughty'.

Some of the key characteristics of the educational and, specifically, the home and family circumstances of the children in these case studies need emphasizing in order to illustrate the overconcentration of exclusion cases in families with a particular background and profile. Educationally there is a major overrepresentation of children with statements of SEN among the case studies, to the tune of almost 20 times their likely occurrence in the whole population. This overrepresentation is many times greater when one considers that the overwhelming majority of the children were statemented for EBD and these children form only a small proportion of those state-mented (national data not available). Socially there is an even greater over-representation of children accommodated by the social services department for a period in the year in which the exclusion(s) took place, who are 500 times more likely to be excluded than average. Stepfamilies were strongly represented among the excluded children living at home, by a factor of four times their expected number. There was a much smaller overrepresentation of lone parents (21 per cent of all households nationally), who made up about a third of the case studies.

There is every reason to believe that these case studies are fairly representative of the kinds of children and circumstances which one might expect to find in the total population of officially excluded primary age children. The next two chapters will explore what parents/carers, children and teachers said about events surrounding the exclusion of such children from school.

Five

Exclusion: the view from home

Carol Hayden and Derek Ward

Background

The last chapter has established factual information on what is known about the children and their home circumstances, as well as basic information about their schooling and history of exclusion. This chapter will be based on qualitative data and will explore the themes which emerged at interview with parents, carers and the children themselves. Interviews with parents, children and key workers were almost always carried out in the children's current place of residence, when they were living with their parents, and in several of the cases, where the child was resident in a children's home. Most social workers were interviewed in their area office. No foster parents were seen because all of the placements were very recent and social services staff advised that contact was not appropriate.

A great deal of thought was put into how to obtain the children's viewpoint about their exclusion(s) in a way which would not be harmful and which might even be enjoyable, for a group of children who had already (in many cases) had a lot of people asking them questions. One issue related to the knowledge that a large proportion of the children came from family circumstances where there was concern about parenting and significant social services involvement. There was thus a very real possibility of child protection issues being raised if the focus of the interview was not carefully defined. For these reasons children were only asked about their exclusion(s) and more general experiences of school. No questions were asked about their parents, siblings or general home circumstances. This was a quite deliberate decision, in order to try and avoid exploring areas which may be both especially painful and contentious and which we felt, as researchers (rather than as practitioners) ill equipped to deal with. Parents/ carers were assured of the focus of the questions which would be asked of children and shown a copy of the children's interview booklet before an interview proceeded. Children too were shown the booklet when they were asked whether they were willing to be interviewed, and they were assured that their teachers, parents and carers would not be told anything about what they said in relation to their exclusion from school. However, it was made clear that if they divulged other information which could indicate that they were being harmed, or were at risk of harm, then it was our duty as adults to tell somebody who was in a position to help them.

This chapter will now focus on how the parents and carers described the children's behaviour, their strategies for behaviour management, their communication with schools and their experience and feelings about the exclusion process. The chapter will then continue with the children's thoughts and feelings about their exclusions.

The children's behaviour

After establishing factual information about the child and family circumstances, parents and carers were asked whether there was anything about the subject's behaviour which caused any difficulty or concern in the home. It was strongly emphasized at this point that we were focusing upon behaviour out of school and their experiences of the child, rather than what others said about the child.

Parents/carers were invited to describe the behaviour of the children out of school and in particular to cite any behaviours which they found problematic. At the end of the interview parents/carers were asked to complete a behaviour rating scale, which was utilized to corroborate evidence about particular behaviours discussed as well as raise issues about behaviours not mentioned during the interview. The rating scales were also analysed in order to identify possible groups of behaviours, known as constructs, which might be viewed as 'disorders' by psychologists. Observations were made at the time of the visit. Utilizing these various ways of collecting data about behaviour meant that a broader picture could be gained of the child's out-of-school behaviour than would be gained from using one data collection technique alone. It was sometimes clear for example that a parent felt that they could cope with the child/ren at home, but recognized that they did things which might be seen as problematic by others or in different situations. In several cases the interview setting itself was a graphic illustration of interactional difficulties in some families.

Social workers and key workers in children's homes (carers) provided the insight into children's behaviour out of school in some cases, although in one case the child's mother, social worker and key worker in the children's home were all seen. All of the children in the care of the local authority were displaying very extreme behaviour, ranging from a child who was on a major tranquilizer to sedate her, to children who were viewed simply as very difficult in their destructive and absconding behaviour. The accounts of carers are reported in a separate subsection below.

Accounts from parents

The parent spoken to was most often the mother of the child, although fathers were the main carers in two cases, alongside a stepmother in one of these cases. Birth fathers were present at two of the interviews, but in each case expected the mother to take the lead in any assessment of the child. In one interview where a stepfather was present, the parents were interviewed separately because they did not agree about a number of issues in relation to the child. Some parents saw the excluded child as somebody who had always been difficult. Only one parent reported no problems at all with her son.

Many of the parents viewed the particular child who was excluded as more difficult than their sibling(s). Sometimes this was largely about relatively minor 'stroppiness', as in the case of Daniel, who had a number of fixed term exclusions. Daniel is the middle child in a family of five children. His mother said of him: 'Daniel has always been difficult, since a small child. He doesn't seem to learn from his mistakes. He's generally got far too much to say for himself as a 12-year-old.' The parents of Gareth, who was permanently excluded from school, said of him:

> He was difficult in playschool and first school . . . he always wants peoples' undivided attention . . . One neighbour has banned him coming round because of his language . . . He runs off and doesn't come back for hours . . . Twice we've had the police out looking for him. He's taken bikes from gardens round here, even though he's got his own. He's very streetwise.

Pippa's mother described her daughter as very difficult and different from her older sister, right from babyhood: 'She was very energetic from the word go, she hardly slept. She's asked for sleeping pills because she knows I take them. Sometimes she stays up all night reading . . . She's manipulative beyond belief.' While it may not be surprising that parents looked to the individual child rather than their home circumstances in explaining the child's behaviour, it was clear that for many parents their child's behaviour was not acceptable to them.

As mentioned in the last chapter, three of the four more affluent parents were sufficiently concerned about their child to pay for a private assessment. One of these children is Thomas, who was in Year 6 at the time of his permanent exclusion. He spent six months out of school before obtaining a place at secondary school. He had moved schools at the end of Year 5, after two fixed term exclusions. His mother described him in the following way:

> Things snowball, something quite trivial happens and it all gets out of hand . . . he does overreact . . . Over the years we've learned to deal with it. I can't put my finger on it . . . It started happening in the second year of juniors [Year 4]. We have never discovered what has caused it . . . We've seen a psychiatrist and she said that something happened, but she couldn't find out what it was.

Nathan was at the start of Year 7 in a middle school at the time of his permanent exclusion. He too had moved schools at the end of the previous school year because of difficulties there, which included exclusions. Nathan's mother was so concerned about the older children he was spending time with out of school that the family moved house a sufficient distance to sever the friendships. Nathan's mother believed that he had been glue sniffing. He had a private assessment from a psychologist. However, Nathan's mother was positive about the work Nathan's home tutor had done with him, particularly in raising his self-esteem by building upon his strengths. She was relieved that he had finally been statemented and would be attending a special school in the next academic year, but annoyed that he still had to go through the lengthy process of formal assessment by the LEA, despite his private assessment.

One parent felt that all of her children were uncontrollable; five children were resident with her, the two older children living with their father. She described them as 'hyperactive' and thought that the younger children were worse than the subject of the interview. Paul was the oldest child living with her. She described her feelings about trying to look after him thus:

> I really don't know what to do, I wanted him to go back to his dad. I felt as if I really can't cope with him . . . I rang his father and said I wanted him to take him. He said he didn't want to take him back, he was trying to get a job. He said he'd have to go into a home, but I couldn't have that . . . I'll just have to put up with it. It's enough for me with the four that I've got without Paul.

Bradley's mother recognized similarities between herself and her son. She had been in children's homes herself as a child but was determined that this should not happen to Bradley. She also blamed Bradley's violent stepfather for many of his emotional and behavioural difficulties.

Although some parents reported that their child was manageable within the family, this often meant only the very immediate family who lived together. For example, the mother of twin 8-year-old boys (Lewis and Jerry) said:

> They are very active, noisy, boisterous, full of life, they eat like horses. They are the same as any other boys their age when we are a family. When we go to a different place or there are other people around, problems can occur. We don't have any problems that we can't cope with as a family.

However, she also reported that they did not get invited round to friends' houses to play and relatives would only have them round if she stayed with them. The parent of another 8-year-old boy (Chris) felt that individually she could cope with him, but acknowledged that he had major problems in coping with groups of people:

> To be quite honest he hasn't got a behaviour problem now . . . you can see the difference since he's been in the new school [a special school] . . . [but] even if I have six or seven people over from the family, he can't cope with it. He'll go and hide under his bed for a couple of hours . . . I knew he wasn't capable of being in school at five, in a class of 32.

Some of the parents saw their child as relatively isolated and without real friends. Shane had been quite aggressive towards his mother in the past, but was said to have settled down at the time of interview. She said of him: 'I really haven't got a problem with Shane . . . He's not very outgoing . . . he likes security. He's a loner . . . he hasn't got any friends.' However, she later described how he would throw things at her and she had to be quick to get out of the way. Apparently this was not viewed as problematic behaviour by Shane's mother. Interestingly it was also the throwing of objects which was seen to be most dangerous by his teacher. For example, he had tried to throw a javelin at another child on one occasion. Other parents reflected a similar ambivalence, while acknowledging that their sons could be aggressive to others, they said they had not been aggressive towards them. However, there was an awareness of potential aggression, as this quote from Henry's mother illustrates: 'He is getting much bigger . . . I look at him and think gosh if you lost your temper now . . . [but] I have never been at the brunt of it.'

Some children were viewed as stubborn and difficult to discipline, but not 'out of control'. Such parents were not greatly worried about their children's behaviour, but were worried about them being out of school and where it may lead. For example, Tony's mother said of her 10-year-old son: 'He started to smoke and he's been caught on a number of occasions and he's quite aggressive at times. I'm just basically worried about what he's doing when he's outside.'

While Jordon's mother was extremely upset about his fixed term exclusions, she felt she had good control over him at home. Nevertheless she expressed concerns for the future, as the disabled single parent of a boy who was viewed as quite aggressive at school. She described him in the following way: 'He's stubborn. He doesn't know when to stop. He won't take "no" for an answer. He doesn't stop when friends ask him to.'

Only in one case did a parent report no concerns or problems with their excluded child, although this parent did acknowledge that her son 'took on' adults in a way she would never have dared to do at his age. This young boy had a number of fixed term exclusions, two of which had resulted in the staff in the school using restraint procedures. Adam's mother described her son thus: 'I think I'm blissfully lucky with him . . . just the normal hassles you have with a growing child.'

Accounts from social services staff

Most of the accounts from social workers were of very extreme behaviour, which was often described as destructive, out of control and aggressive. Some of the behaviour was seen as so severe by others living with the child that the parents and later the foster parents had felt that they could not keep the child.

In the case of Jeremiah the whole family was discharged from a women's refuge because of his behaviour. Jeremiah's mother made a number of requests to have him accommodated by social services, but this did not happen until he stabbed his older brother with a kitchen knife. At the time of fieldwork he had again been returned to his mother because no suitable placement could be found for him.

Charlie was placed with foster parents, one of whom is a teacher at an EBD school. However, the family found it impossible to contain him:

> He was placed in school with the adoptive sister. He wanted to be like his new sister but he was envious of her secure position in the family, he began to leap on her and be aggressive. He frightened her and her friends. The family had to call the police on one occasion because he was uncontrollable. He was admitted to hospital where he had to be physically restrained in order not to hurt himself. [The family] were very reluctant to give up on him but it was doomed . . . he was so aggressive.

In both cases these children were placed in mainstream schools. Jeremiah was later permanently excluded from school. Charlie had so many moves during the 1993–4 school year that he was not attending school for much of the time anyway.

Children who had spent time in local authority care had very disrupted lives, with very inconsistent controls and limits applied by their birth parents, as the case of Sarah illustrates:

> Basically there is no stability at home at all. Mum didn't mind if she went to school . . . if she was on the street until 12 o'clock at night . . . Sarah could do what she wanted to, she was smoking, she knew all the swear words, she could drink . . . she spoke to her mum as she liked . . . and basically got way out of control.

Some children had their confusion and instability compounded, by parents and other relatives fighting over their custody. Katy had spent a lot of time in the care of her grandparents while her mother was in prison. She had also spent time in local authority care. In the year in which she was permanently excluded from school (Year 4) she had been removed from her grandparents into foster care and then placed with her mother, stepfather and five siblings. The grandparents wanted the children to come back and live with them and were encouraging the children's difficult behaviour in the belief that it would be blamed on their mother and that they would be returned to them (the grandparents) to live. Her social worker said of Katy: 'She is an extremely difficult child to manage . . . unpredictable. She would grab other people's things and destroy other children's work. She would knock things over and move things about. She was so wound up and angry.'

Several of the children were destructive with other children's property, and sometimes the property of adults too. Pippa's key worker described her behaviour in the following way: 'Anything that isn't nailed down she will lay claim to. Pippa is destructive towards property, but not her own property, she is very possessive of that, she destroys other children's property or toys.'

Several of the children were described as disturbed in their behaviour, rather than as out of control. Tommy's social worker described a situation which she felt had been terrible from the start, but had also been badly handled by the social services department:

Tommy started nursery [aged 18 months] and proceeded to demolish it . . . It's appalling, we've had him since 1986 and we still haven't settled his future, either by a home or through education . . . He was a disturbed child when he came to us, all we've done is make him worse . . . He constantly attacks adults both physically and verbally.

Catherine's social worker described her as the most disturbed girl she had met: 'Catherine has temper tantrums which can last five to six hours, in which she goes in for lots of self-mutilation. She breaks windows and knocks down doors. She displays lots of disturbed and regressive behaviour, such as sucking a dummy and drinking from a baby's bottle.'

Some social workers were very keen not to label children as 'disturbed', but nevertheless emphasized the extreme nature of the child's behaviour, particularly in terms of the major fluctuations in behaviour displayed.

Home strategies and attitudes towards behaviour management and discipline

As nearly half of the children had spent time in care during the year of their exclusion, they were inevitably subjected to changes in styles of managing their behaviour out of school by their changes of placement. Many of these cases are so complex that it is difficult to make any generalizations at all about the strategies adopted by their birth parents, other than they were usually inconsistent; where parents were interviewed they often reported feeling at a total loss as to what to do. This subsection will therefore only draw upon the interviews with parents. In addition another eight families had social work involvement, which in all but one case related in part to support for the child and parenting skills for the parents, as well as other specific needs in the family. In the case where social services involvement was not focused on parenting there were major concerns from the school about the parents' methods of discipline, which were seen as overly punitive. The school were sufficiently concerned to have been in contact with the social services department about this, early on in the child's school career.

The majority of parents who could report clear strategies tended to focus on punishments, withdrawal of privileges, and 'grounding', rather than rewarding wanted behaviour. It was clear that many of the parents looked to schools to provide stronger discipline and help them 'sort their children out'. Several parents made strong comments on what they felt was the need for stronger punishments in school, in particular corporal punishment.

Levi's mother tried a range of punishments but felt that her son did not respect her as a woman. He did, however, respond to male authority, so she involved her brother in punishing him:

> I've tried all sorts of things. I take away his games or whatever he likes to do. I take away things that he likes doing. I smack him. I've always smacked him . . . my brother is involved now, he's quite strict. He will come and have a talk with him or give him some punishment, like facing the wall, putting his hands up . . . Levi tends to respond to male more than female figures and at school they don't have a male teacher.

The theme about lack of male authority figures in primary school was raised by several parents of boys at interview. Nathan's mother reported feeling 'stunned' at the lack of disciplinary options schools have. She had said to the school, 'if you want to restrain Nathan, you've got my permission'. The head teacher had said to her, 'I can't, Mrs Johns, not even with your permission.' She went on to say that she felt that children had 'too many rights' and recounted a story where the child's father had hit him in public around the head and one of the child's friends had called the police. The police warned the father. Nathan's mother felt that the whole situation compounded her difficulties with him, as he now had the impression that adults could not stop him from doing whatever he wanted.

There was some criticism of the way schools disciplined children. Occasionally this was a very specific criticism about the strategy a particular teacher was using, which was the source of conflict between parent and school in some cases. In other cases parents reported their confusion about the idea of rewarding appropriate behaviour, and the nature of and rationale behind sanctions used in schools. This confusion, and sometimes criticism, like the case above, was often highly personal in the sense that parents were sometimes torn between wanting their child to be shown more understanding yet also stronger discipline in school.

Disagreement between parents about methods of discipline was not uncommon. Often mothers were trying to protect their sons from a father, or stepfather, who was seen as more disciplinarian. Sometimes the protection was because of a disagreement about methods of discipline and other times it was because the mother had sympathy with the child and wanted to protect them. 'I gave up!' said Ian's mother. She explained that Ian's father tended to shout and just 'blow up'. She said of her son, 'I do tend to side with him, but his dad does go on about things the wrong way sometimes.'

A minority of parents reported putting on a united front. For example, Thomas's mother said:

> We are very firm with him, we don't let anything go. We have sanctions which we can apply, such as he misses his favourite television programme, we stop his pocket money, he's not allowed out to play. They work at home . . . We try to give a united front . . . I think that is important. I don't like the idea of him playing one of us off against the other.

The mother of the twin boys, Lewis and Jerry, reported 'showing a united front' with the children's stepfather, as well as working with the school, to try and produce a consistent approach to their behaviour.

Some parents tried to keep their child/ren out of the way: for example in two families the children were not allowed to share the lounge with their parents, but were expected go to their room, sometimes straight after school. One such child was taken into care, another had a brief period in respite care, with ongoing work with the stepmother and father. Such parents clearly were desperate for some support and advice, but were not always keen to go to social services for it. Paul's mother said the idea of taking her children out for the day in the summer holidays was something she just could not cope with. She said they had no sense of danger, they would just run off in all directions or start throwing stones and similar activities.

Home–school relationship and communication

Before asking specifically about the child's exclusion, the interviews with parents and carers tried to explore the issues of home–school relationships and communications of concern and support for the child in question. Parents' accounts could be very ambivalent. Sometimes this seemed to relate to the sheer upset of having a young child with whom a school was unable (or unwilling) to cope and sometimes it related to the parents' own attitudes towards and experiences of education. Some parents reported a lack of confidence about contacting the school or other parts of the education service, others said the whole process of having their child excluded from school left them feeling powerless.

Relationships between social services staff and school were very varied, although there was remarkably little criticism of teachers and schools in the cases investigated. Social services staff were certainly frustrated with the education system, however, and some reported the difficulty of getting some children into another school after they had been excluded. Many showed an appreciation of the realities of trying to cater for the child in a school, not least because it created extra problems for them if the child was out of school. This was particularly so for key workers in children's homes, who sometimes had the main responsibility for the children all day for months if they were permanently excluded from school, apart from a few hours home tuition a week.

Comments from parents

Parents comments about home–school relations and communication were very wide ranging. Clearly some parents thought they were continually being contacted in relation to their child and felt that schools should know what to do with them during the school day. In other words, they did not welcome either the amount or kind of communication they were getting from the school. Several parents felt they were continually called up to the school because of their child's behaviour. Jordon's mother said: 'I was basically called up to the school every time something happened.' Levi's mother was getting a daily report on her son. She felt this was too often: 'They've fed [back] . . . to me on a daily basis. Sometimes I don't think that's such a good idea because I think it should be an overall picture, rather than he's good today, tomorrow he's not . . . he has a report book which is supposed to come home daily.'

In contrast, other parents wanted more communication. One parent (herself a teacher) felt that communication with the school was not very good. She said they did not get in touch until there was a crisis. The parents asked for a daily report system to be implemented, but this never happened. One parent described how a head teacher did not follow the proper procedures: 'a lot of meetings were held at which I should have been present'. The education welfare officer helped her to write to a parent governor asking why correct procedure had not been adhered to.

On the other hand, there was a sense of frustration for some parents who just wanted their child to be able to stay in school all day, but did not want to be constantly consulted about it. Nathan's mother described the practical difficulties of both parents working full-time and having to deal with calls from the school. At one meeting with the head teacher she reported herself as saying: 'I said to them, he's in school, you should be able to control him. They said "We can't do anything." In my day you wouldn't dare do it. They're not even allowed to grab a child's arm . . . to me its gone right the other way, they push it back on the parents.' A few parents felt that their child was not listened to and that they too were not properly talked with over the incident.

Chris had been permanently excluded twice by the time he started a special school at the age of 8. His mother was very concerned to avoid problems and went into his new school on the first day. She said: 'I was so afraid that this was his last chance, that I asked the headmaster whether I could be in the classroom or be around to see what they were doing.' The school said they did not think it was appropriate that she should help in the same classroom as her son, but would like to include her as a volunteer elsewhere in the school, which they did. She reported gaining insight into how to manage her son's behaviour from this work and said she did the work for herself as much as the children she was helping. The school also have a daily diary system which both the teacher and parent fill in. A term into this new placement, both parent and child talked very positively about this special school – they both felt they knew where they were and understood the system. Importantly, Chris's mother felt included by the school and that she was learning to help other children, as well as Chris.

Bradley's mother was appreciative of his school, even though he was only attending part-time at the time of interview. She said: 'They've supported me through thick and thin . . . it's just that the school isn't equipped to cope with children with behavioural disorders . . . He should be in school full-time, but with what they have to put up with I can't blame them for not having him there all day.' Pippa was permanently excluded from school and yet her mother was similarly appreciative of the school's efforts with her daughter: 'I've never seen a school put as much effort into a child as they put into her . . . My total heart goes out to them. That head teacher is dedicated to her job, she really is . . . it's a good school as well.'

Although many parents and carers felt that the school had put a lot of time into a particular child, there was sometimes disagreements between parents. For example, one child's father opened the interview with a comment relating to schools being concerned about performance and wanting to exclude troublemakers. The mother then said the school had done a lot for Gareth and 'put up with a lot of shit from him'. The child's mother had spent time in school supporting the child, as she had done in his first school. These parents believed that the child needed more discipline but looked to the school to provide it during the school day. They reported feeling nervous as parents as to how they should discipline their children. They said of the exclusion meeting at the school: 'They didn't have a clue what to do with him . . . being teachers, that surprised me. They wanted him out of the way.'

Only a minority of parents mentioned a particular teacher or head teacher not liking their child. Sometimes parents felt that this extended to them, which made constructive communication extremely difficult. As the parent of a Year 7 boy said: 'Daniel has been a problem, I don't think the head teacher likes him, which is understandable. But in the position he holds he shouldn't be down to just the head teacher to decide on a suspension.' The parent of Rajah, a Year 6 boy permanently excluded from school, said: 'From the word go he didn't hit it off with the teacher . . . The teacher was picking on him as soon as he started that school. At the time his aunty had just died. I had explained it to the school, they need to understand that children have feelings the same as them.'

Some parents were not sure what happened or why, in relation to their child's exclusion. For example the mother of Paul, a permanently excluded child who was living with his father at the time of the exclusion, said: 'I don't really know why he was thrown out.' Paul was in receipt of a draft statement at the time of interview. The date on the document was some two months before and had originally been sent to his father's house. Paul's mother did not understand the significance of the document, and although it was almost the end of the school year, was not sure whether or not her son had a place at secondary school. He had already had a whole year out of school by this time. She needed help, which we gave her, with understanding the document and knowing who to contact at the education office. She clearly felt powerless to make changes in her situation and was very fearful of the future for her younger children. They were about to start the junior school from which Paul was excluded. She said of them: 'They don't want to go there. They know what Paul went through. I've just told them they have to go there, that they'll have to behave themselves . . . but I'm just waiting for it to happen to them.'

Jordon's mother went to the same church as the head teacher of her son's voluntary aided school. She was very supportive of the school ethos and had helped the school in practical ways. She was extremely upset by his exclusions and felt that her son had been seen as a problem 'from day one'. Like Paul's mother, she also felt powerless to change the situation and fearful for the future. She said: 'I get tense as soon as the school term starts, and every day when I go to pick him up, I wonder what they're going to say he's done.'

Parents, like Jordon's mother, just wanted everything to be alright and for their child to stay in a school where they knew people, although sadly the term 'friends' could not be used in many cases. If a school was perceived to be 'good', parents were very reluctant to consider taking their child elsewhere and were particularly worried that they might not have any choice about the matter.

The mother of twin boys on an indefinite exclusion described going to a meeting to decide whether they were going to be integrated back into the school: 'I was thoroughly beaten down by that meeting because they were all professionals and I wasn't. I came out of the meeting to find they'd been excluded and I had to take them straight home.'

Comments from social services staff

Interviews with social services staff were less emotionally charged than those with parents; the impact and significance of the child's exclusion for these carers was inevitably coloured by their perception of the role of social services staff in relation to the education of children in their care. Education was often not the top priority when an appropriate home environment was being sought or developed. However, having the children out of school could create practical difficulties for some staff and could lead to periods of respite care for children living with parents and breakdowns in foster placements, as well as additional responsibility for key workers in children's homes.

Some social services staff were trying to make good links with schools, not least to try and help keep children in school, as the following quote illustrates: 'As the situation became more difficult I made regular contact with the school, as a social worker I believe that is part of my job.'

In recognition that the parents of many of the children in local authority care may be unable or unwilling to support their children in school, some social services staff actually spent time in the classroom with children, in order to keep them in school. A key worker in a children's home said:

> There wasn't any contact between home and school, as far as I'm aware of because mum didn't want to know . . . The school were prepared to take her back as long as they got the support. It was the support that they needed . . . [our] staff are sitting with these children in school. A lot of the kids are putting themselves on report to show us they're doing alright.

However, this key worker did not want her line manager to know how much time she was spending with Katy in school, as she feared this would not be approved of.

Although exclusion was an unwelcome event it was never a total surprise to social services staff. For example, Catherine's social worker said that the exclusion was not a sudden event. She described the relationship between the school and the foster carers as good, so that when Catherine had distressed days they would come and collect her and take her home. The social services department were already looking for a therapeutic placement: 'There was no precipitous event. I think they wanted to hold on to her, they were as committed as they could be. There was a lot of aggression towards staff. The atmosphere in the school with the other children was difficult and not doing Catherine any good.'

One social worker commented that liaison between a particular special school and social workers was good and that the previous head was good at liaising and listening. However, at the time of Tommy's exclusion this head teacher was off work on long-term sick leave. She said of the acting head teacher: 'He was stressed, my god . . . he was stressed out of his brains really. That school is supposed to be equipped to deal with people like Tommy, maybe they're asking too much of them.'

Social workers were sometimes surprised how much effort some schools were willing to put into extremely challenging children: 'I felt that particular school had done a heck of a lot more than I'd seen any other school willing to do.'

Some social services staff recognized that certain children could be extremely difficult in a mainstream classroom and that pressure on the head teacher to exclude could come from parents of other children:

> I must say that I think the school worked very hard to try and help Charlie. He was excluded for short periods two or three times for the same reasons, grabbing little girls and touching their genitalia . . . [the head teacher] knowing his history and knowing that we were looking

for an adoptive family, she didn't want his record spoilt by expelling him, but she was under pressure from the parents of the girls.

On the other hand some social work staff perceived whole-school behaviour policies as potentially unhelpful to the more volatile children in their care. The key worker of Joe, a Year 6 boy permanently excluded from school said:

> We did what we could as carers of Joe. We were as responsive as we could be. The education support service were called in at the first sign of difficulties which we felt we couldn't handle . . . but the headmaster seemed to have made up his mind. The school didn't appear to have anything to put on the table and wasn't prepared to make an exception with Joe . . . Assertive Discipline seemed to gradually grind him down.

There were, however, some instances where social services staff admitted not telling a school about the level of difficulty in a child's background, because they believed the school would not offer the child a place if they knew the full story:

> The head of the children's home decided that a new school wouldn't take him if they knew of his record, so she arranged a place without telling the school anything. The first weeks at the school were problematic with Steve presenting great difficulties. However, the school appears to be containing him at present.

These sorts of admissions were evident to schools and could lead to less than welcoming responses to social workers trying to help a child obtain a school place.

Experiencing the exclusion of a child from school

Parents rather more than carers looked for an explanation for why their child had been excluded from school. Explanations tended to focus on the individual child more often than the school. However, parents' experiences of dealing with schools were very varied, as the earlier accounts illustrate, and many interviewees were well aware of resource issues, such as the hours brought by a statement. Some individuals were also well aware of the possible effect of a more market-orientated education system.

Some parents very definitely believed their child to be misplaced in mainstream education. In two cases parents had kept their children off school because they felt the provision made in mainstream schooling for their sons was not suitable. In one case the LEA had threatened prosecution because of the child's non-attendance. One of these parents described how she kept her son (Chris) at home until he was $5\frac{1}{2}$ years old before allowing him to go to school; he was permanently excluded by the age of 6. He then went to a special unit for two years, where his mother reported that 'he got on brilliantly'. He was put back into a mainstream school in an unplanned way and was out again in a matter of weeks: 'I honestly believe it's about the number of children in the class. He's in a small group now . . . It's a shame that every school hasn't got a class for the children who can't behave and can't keep up . . . to help them.'

Bradley had only been attending school part-time for much of Year 2. He was assessed at an EBD special unit after he was permanently excluded. Initially the unit did not want to take Bradley because they thought his needs were too severe. However, his mother appealed against the decision and he was then placed in the unit. Bradley's mother said of his mainstream school: 'They haven't got what Bradley needs . . . He's emotionally disturbed . . . I know that, I've known that for a long time. He's getting therapy . . . In school he loses concentration really quickly, then up his books will go and he'll start rolling around the floor, kicking and screaming.'

Pippa's mother was adamant that it was Pippa as an individual who was the issue. She saw her as very intelligent and unusually strong and energetic. She was very supportive of the education system more generally. Her biggest worry was the amount of time her daughter was out of school. Pippa was in the care of the local authority both at the time of her exclusion and for months afterwards. The plan was to reunite her with her mother. Pippa's mother said of the situation:

> I still do not accept that there is anything wrong at home. Pippa is a violent child who needs restraining . . . she's slashed all of my carpets, she slashed the quilt with a stanley knife . . . I believe her problems come from education. Her biggest problems at the moment are that she is not being educated . . . Without education she's got no future.

Pippa's mother was pleased that she was going to start at a special school the next academic year.

For some parents/carers the actual event of an exclusion was unexpected, whether or not they had previously been warned by the head teacher that it was possible or even likely, partly because of the young age of their child. Some parents expressed surprise and frustration that they could be prosecuted for their child's non-attendance at school, yet they did not have the right to immediate access to another facility, should their child be excluded from school.

Many of the parents reported feeling abandoned, with very limited access to support or advice about what to do. Lewis and Jerry's mother described the situation very succinctly:

> When these children are thrown out, you are literally dumped on the wayside until somebody thinks 'Oh they've been out for six months . . . we'd better do something about it.' They're like two bad apples in a barrel. They've been left rotting away for too long . . . There's got to be some intermediate thing . . . in between being in or out. There should be something there on a Tuesday if they are thrown out on a Monday.

The effect of exclusion on children and their families naturally varied in relation to the type of exclusion the child had, as well as the families' reaction to it, among other variables. At best lives were merely disrupted, at worst the exclusion was viewed as a major catastrophe. The power of an event like exclusion to add to and even precipitate further problems is difficult to predict. In some cases a permanent exclusion was part of the scenario at home which helped bring about a period of time in the care of the local authority, for certain children.

When Kevin was permanently excluded his stepmother found it very difficult to cope with him:

> He was too much for me . . . I wouldn't let him out to play . . . I was trying to set him work. [Then] I started laying into him, I'm not proud of it, I thought I might really hurt him . . . I was in pieces the day he went into respite [in short term care of the local authority] . . . I said I don't want him to go now . . . he needed a break from me. The poor child went through hell.

For other parents even a fixed term exclusion was a devastating event: 'I was so angry, I just went home to bed and slept . . . Jordon wasn't at fault . . . He just sat in here [the living room] and watched television . . . I feel like killing myself. I'm a total nervous wreck.' This parent was about to take an extended holiday in Africa with her son because she wanted to escape the whole situation.

Several parents mentioned feeling that they were being punished and it certainly curtailed the activities of some parents, who had to give up work for a period or abandon studying and training. One such parent who had to abandon plans to work part-time said: 'I hate him being home . . . I feel like I'm being punished . . . it's a holiday for him.'

Some parents felt confused about how they should treat their child, especially if they were at home for some time. One parent described the initial effect of having her 10-year-old son, Thomas, permanently excluded from school as 'shattering' for the whole family, but said that over the months they had built up a new routine around the home tuition. This parent had to give up her supply teaching work for a period after Thomas's exclusion and was still clearly very shaken by the event at interview some months later. However, home tuition was not always offered very quickly and some children got into the habit of doing very little. Some parents deliberately kept their excluded child in the house during school hours.

An additional worry and consideration for parents was the potential effect of an exclusion on the excluded child's siblings and the rest of the family. Sometimes other children in a family worried about going to the same school as their excluded sibling (for example Paul's siblings referred to on p. 76). Siblings sometimes wanted to spend time at home. One parent described how the exclusion of her twin boys (Lewis and Jerry) seemed to dominate the whole family: 'We wanted to get them into a school where they'd come home at the end of the day and everybody had a nice day

– the boys, the teachers, other children . . . all we were doing at one point was talking about Jerry and Lewis, if you're not careful it takes over everything.' This parent also had to give up her further education course because of the disruption of having her two sons at home every lunchtime all year, as well as periods of fixed term and indefinite exclusion.

Most of the parents reported negative effects of the longer term exclusions on their child. Some parents went as far as describing their child as 'depressed'. Chris's two permanent exclusions had meant he had spent about six months each time out of school. Chris was referred to in the preface. He had suffered some very severe bullying from children in the neighbourhood, so his mother would not let him out to play when other children were around. Consequently he was very restricted and lacked any opportunity for stimulation. Some months into the exclusion under investigation, the NSPCC became involved with the family and provided some support and activities for the child.

Even though Bradley was attending school part-time at the time of interview, he still felt excluded, both because of his part-time exclusion and what was in effect an internal exclusion. His mother said:

> I didn't like the fact that he was excluded from school. It isn't good for him. He is certainly not learning to mix with his peer group, which is one of his problems . . . [when he's in school] he never goes into his class anyway. He feels excluded, he feels alone. He understands why he has been excluded, but it doesn't help him.

Some children were said to be worried about missing out on school and mentioned this in the separate interviews with them. One parent believed that the whole experience of permanent exclusion had been deeply upsetting to her son: 'I think what Henry made of the experience was not conscious . . . He used to get up every night for three months crying and screaming. He didn't remember it the next day. I just used to cuddle him and cuddle him.'

Many children were reported to be upset about being excluded and recognized it as a very significant event. This was sometimes the case even when the exclusion was only for a day or so, as Dale's mother reported: 'He was upset about being excluded . . . it shook him up because it was an exclusion, that was something. He had to have been really naughty to get excluded.' Other children were less upset or worried, particularly about fixed term exclusion, at the outset at least. However, if a child had a series of fixed term exclusions it did tend to worry them.

It was obvious to many parents that their child was bored, if they were excluded for any length of time. It was extremely difficult for parents to provide enough stimulation and variety during the day. Many parents did not like their children to be outside unsupervised during the school day, for a variety of reasons. Some parents thought that it simply was not right, that their child should be in school. Others were fearful of what they might get up to or whom they might meet. A few parents did not want their neighbours to know that their child was out of school. For many children this left them with the television and often a computer for stimulation. Ian's mother's comment is fairly typical: 'He was really quite bored when he was first sent home . . . but he got used to it. He has his computer upstairs.'

Comments from social services staff

Many of the comments from social services staff echoed those of parents. Some children were viewed as inappropriately placed in mainstream education and even in day special schools. In several cases (such as Catherine, Charlie and Andrew), staff said that these children were in need of a residential therapeutic environment, yet two of these children had been in mainstream education at the time of their exclusion from school. Children were sometimes described as not emotionally 'fit' to go to school anyway at the time of their exclusion (such as Pippa). Children were often difficult to occupy, although staff in children's homes would try to set up activity programmes for the children to supplement home tuition. Some social workers would also take the children out on occasion. Their reactions to this additional responsibility ranged from anger that the education service did not provide an adequate alternative schooling for such young children, to an acceptance that there simply were not enough suitable facilities. Some social services staff recognized the difficulties in finding appropriate staff when home tuition was the only option available.

What the children said

Twenty-two children were available and willing to be interviewed. This subsample is broadly representative of the case studies as a whole in many respects, such as age range, ethnicity and evidence of special educational needs. However, it was only possible to interview one of the girls because of the very volatile and sensitive circumstances in the other four cases of excluded girls. Also, a slightly higher proportion of the children had experienced a permanent exclusion than is the case in the whole sample. The children's responses will be presented in four main themes: getting excluded; time out of school; going back to school; and school rules, rewards and sanctions.

Getting excluded

For the majority of the children exclusion was an event that was significant and remembered even if the time out of school was only a matter of days. The children knew that it was an unusual event for somebody of their age, and again the majority could describe which behaviours had led to their exclusion. A common theme throughout the interviews with children was the child recalling an incident which related to physical altercations with other pupils or adults. Children emphasized these events more than their parents and even more than their teachers.

Jerry describes a key event before one of his exclusions: 'I was being naughty and silly . . . I wasn't doing as I was told and I kicked someone in the leg . . . five times.' Peter was talking about a previous permanent exclusion when he said: 'I wasn't allowed to go to school for pushing a girl down the stairs.' (She broke her ankle.) Shamus had a number of fixed term exclusions, all for fighting. He said that the reason for his exclusion was: 'I used to have fights at school . . . about one a day.' Gareth, who was permanently excluded, thought it was 'because I kicked the teacher'.

Levi had a fixed term exclusion after an event at lunchtime which he described in the following way: 'I was fighting, it took four teachers to calm me down. They said that I pushed the dinner lady down the stairs.' Chris was given a fixed term exclusion within weeks of starting a mainstream school, after leaving a special unit. He described the behaviour which led to this exclusion thus: 'I was always beating them up [other children] . . . I liked hiding in places where they [the teachers] couldn't find me. One day I ran out of school and didn't go back . . . [he continued] I got told off at school for headbutting the teacher.'

Other children focused on other events. For example Tony was permanently excluded from school after a long period of very difficult behaviour culminating in an allegation of attempted arson. However, he chose to focus on other behaviours in his recall of why he was excluded: 'I was naughty. I was rude, smashing windows and going on the [school] roof.' Kevin said he was excluded because: '[I was] throwing chairs around the classroom . . . I hanged out of the upstairs window. I kept doing that.'

Using a series of smiley faces and thought bubbles, an attempt was made to gain an impression of how the child remembered feeling when they were told they were excluded from school. There was a range of responses. Half the children said they felt angry at being excluded. Anger centred on not being able to go to school and being separated from friends. Five children reported feeling sad, although they could not always articulate why. Two of the older children had a clear sense that evidence against them was building up and did not like this. The same number of children reported not feeling anything about being excluded. Possibly the 'neutral' response was more indicative of conflicting thoughts and feelings, where no single response was dominant. Significantly, only one child associated the exclusion with feelings of happiness. This child was one of the oldest children in the sample. However, two other children also recalled feeling happy but in conjunction with angry feelings. When Nathan was asked why he felt happy at being permanently excluded, he said: 'I just felt like . . . well that's it. I'm going to get some petrol and burn down the school. I just went mental. I wanted to go to school for my education . . . [but] I was happy when I left because the school was too small.'

It is interesting to note that although Nathan talks about being happy about being excluded his comments still reveal a lot of anger about the situation. The overall impression from these interviews with children is that they generally felt angry or sad when told of their exclusion. They had a sense that missing school was not a good thing, probably partly because of what their parents and carers had said to them.

The significance of the event to the children was emphasized by the fact that they could all remember who had informed them that they were to be excluded. Many of the children became very animated at this question and gave a clear account of who told them, what was said and where in the school it occurred.

The children were asked if they thought the exclusion was 'fair'. An attempt was made to elicit the child's perception of the concept of 'fairness'. The children generally appeared to perceive the word in the justice sense. Due to the inherent ambiguity of the term, the children's responses were very varied. While talking with the children and probing their initial response, several children presented their rationale as to why they thought it was fair, unfair or the reasons as to why they were unsure. A minority of the children thought the exclusion was fair. The rationale underpinning these responses was primarily associated with the 'rights and wrongs' of their behaviour. However, a greater number of children felt that in some way their exclusion had not been fair. Reasons included the child feeling they had been unfairly blamed or treated with regard to a particular incident. Some children said their needs were not addressed, that is they had an awareness of their 'special needs'. On the other hand several children appeared to acknowledge that their behaviour warranted some action, but not an exclusion.

Time out of school

The majority of children could recall what they did when they were out of school, with only two children saying they had no recollection. The vast majority of children said that they stayed indoors with their parent, usually their mother, and played computer games or watched television. Most children said they found these activities boring after a while. It was apparent that the children did not spend long periods out of the home during the school day and were generally supervised most of the time. A typical response might be that from Shane, who was at home for six months after his permanent exclusion: 'I helped my mum cleaning . . . I played with my Mega-Drive. I never went out.' Or, as Henry, another permanently excluded child said: 'I didn't do anything really. I stayed indoors with my mum. I just laid down and watched TV.'

Only a minority of children mentioned that they were expected to do some schoolwork. Two children who had fixed term exclusions mentioned that they felt they were punished at home for being excluded.

Children reported a range of feelings about being out of school, with feelings of anger being quite frequent. Most children expressed concern about getting behind with their schoolwork. Six of the children were permanently excluded and out of school at the time of interview. With this group of children there was no indication that any of them perceived non-attendance in a positive manner. One of the children stated that they felt happier at home than in their old school but wanted to go back to a new school. Similar sentiments were expressed by those children who were actually attending school. The degree of negativity associated with non-attendance did appear slightly more pronounced for those children who had experienced several subsequent periods of time out of school. However, a comment by Henry expresses the distress that some of the children appeared to have experienced. He described his feelings at the time after his previous permanent exclusion: 'I'd wish I was at school and I'd think . . . please, please, please let there be another school.'

Although there appeared to be an overall negative feeing towards being out of school, there was also some evidence that for those children who had experienced several periods of exclusion, that they were beginning to accept the position with some resignation.

The issue of peer contact was seen as being important to the children. More than half the children saw their friends while they were out of school. However, a group of children did not see any friends while they were out of school. This situation led to strong feelings and comments from the children. It became apparent in conversation that access to the peer network was very important to the children. If a child had contact with their peer network while they were out of school, the impact of missing peer contact during the school day seemed to be reduced. For those children who did not have contact with their school peers either inside or outside of the school, their exclusion from this contact was keenly felt.

Going back to school

In many ways it was surprising how the great majority of the children were positive about going back to school. Most of them had experienced more than one exclusion and a lot of difficulty and disruption in relation to their schooling and yet they managed to be optimistic about their actual or proposed return to school. For example Shane was about to start secondary school after six months at home: 'I really want to go to senior school, for the art, science, sport and drama. I'm ready. I'm up to it.' Nathan was also moving on to secondary education in a special school after over two school terms at home. His view of this was: 'I can't really wait . . . because it's better education at school, you learn more things than you do in one hour [with a home tutor].'

Peter attended a special unit after a permanent exclusion from a mainstream school. He also had a number of fixed term exclusions from the special unit. However, these exclusions were less of an issue for him, he was very positive about attending a special unit:

> I feel better now because I have lots more friends, I like it because I'm in a special unit. There are about nine or ten kids in the class because I've got special needs. They help me with anything really . . . if I've

got stuck I put up my hand and the teachers come and help you . . . I like being in a special unit . . . it's quieter and you can get on with your work.

Only one child, who was out of school at the time of interview, declined to comment on his thoughts about returning to school. Further conversation revealed that he did not really realize that returning to school was an option. The majority of children said they were happy to go back to school. In one case, Chris ticked the happy face in the interview booklet 14 times, stating when asked that this represented the amount of happiness he felt at going back to school.

What was evident from the responses to the question about their feelings about returning to school was that no child said they felt angry or sad about their actual or future return to school. Further analysis of these responses did find indications that the child's feelings may have been dependent upon whether they were returning to the school which had excluded them, or a new school.

Given three options: return to their old school; go to a new school; or not go to school, only one child opted for not attending school. A few children opted for remaining at their old school, but the majority opted for going to a new school. A key reason for these choices related to peer group. Some children wanted to return to their old school so that they could be with their friends, while some of the children who would prefer to go to a new school wanted to do so in order to avoid contact with their old peer group. Teachers' attitudes towards them featured, but not to a great extent; more so with the older children. The concern was that teachers may not give them a fair chance and would be particularly attentive to their behaviour.

School rules, sanctions and rewards

The final part of the interviews with children involved the showing of a series of pictures which depicted various aspects of the school day. The first picture was of a general classroom scene. This was followed by a series of three pictures which showed a child arriving in a classroom; a child participating in a classroom discussion; and a child speaking directly to a teacher who is sitting at a desk. The aim of these pictures was to present a stimuli around which the child could talk freely about their feelings and thoughts towards certain aspects of school.

The children illustrated a clear understanding of what might be acceptable or unacceptable behaviour in a classroom and towards a teacher. Behaviours which the children routinely identified as 'naughty' included yelling at the teacher, running out of the classroom and not doing your work when told to do so. Nearly half of the children actually identified themselves with the children who were misbehaving. For example, Shane described the classroom scene thus: 'They are doing what I do . . . muck about . . . bash up people's models . . . be stupid . . . make stupid remarks.'

All the children who were prepared to talk about the pictures showed a good understanding of behaviour which was likely to lead to trouble and behaviour which would be seen as 'good' by teachers, such as putting up your hand to ask questions. Most children were aware of the sanctions in their school for not doing what was expected of them. They mentioned the system of report books, ticks on the board and detentions as fair sanctions. However, some of the older children showed an awareness that these sanctions could have limited effects if they chose not to be bound by them.

The procedure of obtaining merits for 'good' behaviour was noted by the majority of children. Nearly all the children were able to identify behaviours which were likely to result in an award or certificate. This strategy found universal support from the children interviewed, with many of them being keen to give examples of their merit awards. There did, however, appear to be some confusion among certain children, a confusion also expressed by their parents and carers, in relation to being given a merit award around the time of their exclusion, with one child expressing surprise that he was given the 'best boy' award the day before he was excluded.

During the course of the interview the children were asked more specifically about the nature of the discipline system at their school. The majority of the children identified being sent out of class as the most common strategy they had experienced. This was usually associated with visits to the head teacher's office for a formal talking to. When asked whether these strategies had changed their behaviour in school, most children said it had not. In some cases, the use of report books home had more impact. One child clearly identified the fact that if his father saw his report book and it contained misdemeanours, that would stop him misbehaving. However, all the children had clearly gone through the spectrum of sanctions and it was perhaps rather difficult for them to decide what may get them to behave appropriately in school.

Thus, while nearly all the children excluded could associate their exclusion with some specific misbehaviour or incident in school, their attitude towards and control over their behaviour is difficult to gauge. Two children said their exclusions had made them behave differently in school, with one child saying it was his 'last chance' when he went back. However, it would appear that for many of the children the actual exclusion, while clearly remembered, had not been instrumental in altering how the child presented in school. This is borne out by the fact that all but one of the children interviewed had continued to experience further disruptions in their schooling.

Summary and conclusions

All but one of the parents and all of the social services staff described the children's behaviour as problematic for adults, although not always dramatically so. Most parents already had to cope with a number of difficulties, and the event of exclusion imposed extra stress on them, as well as the child. The research evidence in this chapter illustrates that children's 'acting out' behaviours are likely to relate to many of the stresses in their home circumstances, as well as any stresses within the school environment. Not all children react to stress in the same way: some children have more effective coping strategies and carry on functioning sufficiently to stay in school, while other children may react with more passive behaviours which present less of a challenge for schools. Upton (1981) has shown that children's behaviour is marked more by change than continuity. Thus the reactions of adults to a child's symptoms of stress are important in either helping to alleviate it or consolidate it into a more lasting state (Galloway 1985). Peagram (1993) proposes the use of the concepts of 'emotional fitness' and 'emotional elasticity', which refer to the ability of children to adapt to different situations and behave appropriately. Extremes of stress can effect a child's emotional fitness and elasticity. The effects of extreme stress on children do not have to be lasting if they are understood and managed appropriately (Galloway *et al.* 1982), yet some parents/carers and indeed teachers may not themselves have the emotional fitness to do this.

Parents especially, and carers to some extent, showed some ambivalence about the role of the school. Generally parents and carers looked to schools to contain and look after their children for six and a half hours a day, there was an expectation that somehow they should be able to do it. At the same time parents and carers often acknowledged that schools and teachers had a difficult job in trying to contain and even teach some of these children. Broadly speaking, we were surprised by the relative lack of criticism about schools from parents/carers and children. For a significant group of parents, school and the education system was viewed as an environment which was difficult to access and understand. For some it was a matter of indifference.

Interviews with children showed exclusion to be a significant event for them. They clearly missed contact with their peer group more than anything, although some children showed an awareness that they were missing their academic education. Children out of school for any length of time were not surprisingly bored and lacking in stimulation. In addition many children were restricted in their movements during the school day by their parents. Parents were often confused about how to manage the event. Yet despite their negative experiences of exclusion and all that went before it, almost all the children out of school were hopeful about their return to school.

The next chapter will explore the circumstances in the schools at the time of the exclusions, as well as the accounts given about these children by their head and class teachers.

Six

Exclusion: the view from schools

Background

Many of the schools and teachers, like the families visited, had particular stresses and difficulties. The most common ones were age range reorganization in schools, with a consequent loss of funding; difficulties in the management structure which included staff turnover and problems of staff recruitment as well as illness; and inadequacies in school buildings. While acknowledging the stresses upon excluding schools, we will not dwell upon them here, nor catalogue them to the extent undertaken in relation to the circumstances of families. Teachers are professionals trained and paid to teach children, and in this sense may be expected to have more options and strategies open to them than individual families. Furthermore there is no comparative data for all of these details about schools in the LEAs studied.

We already know from earlier chapters that children are excluded from school for some aspect or aspects of their behaviour, which the head teacher and often the class teacher find 'unacceptable'. The work of Hargreaves *et al.* (1975) and others have illustrated that the way teachers view their pupils is not without problems. There are many reasons why it is difficult to obtain objective measures of what 'unacceptable behaviour' is and the frequency of its occurrence in schools. One reason is that teachers will differ in their tolerance of particular behaviours, as well as the allowances they may make for particular groups or individual children. Teachers will differ in their ability, confidence and experience in dealing with particular individuals and behaviours. There will be differences between teachers within schools and between schools. Another important issue in relation to teachers and schools is their willingness to report upon difficulties they are having. This operates on two levels. As Badger (1985: 9) has observed, at the level of the individual teacher the whole issue of classroom management can be a very sensitive area: 'historically, throughout much of the educational world, the individual classroom teacher is left to find his or her own salvation. Failure to do so, carries an often thinly veiled interpolation from some colleagues of inadequacy and weakness.'

At the level of the school, it can be assumed that no head teacher wants to make official reports about all the problems in their school, particularly in a context of the marketization of the education service. Not only will governors get to hear about the problems (some of whom are likely to be parents of children in the school) but information about permanent exclusions is made public by OFSTED inspection. Thus what is reported upon here is the behaviours which class and head teachers found sufficiently 'unacceptable' that exclusion from school was deemed the appropriate sanction. It is interesting to reflect upon what the fact of reporting an exclusion to the LEA may mean to a head teacher. It may be that publicity about the issue of exclusion has raised awareness in head teachers that they should be following set procedures and report exclusions to the governing body and the LEA, when previously they did not. It may be that head teachers are building up a case for formal assessment for special educational needs and more resources to address a child's needs. It may be that children are perceived as presenting more difficult behaviour than at some time previously in a head teacher's teaching career – whether this perception is accurate or not. It may be that reported exclusions are a real indicator of unmet special educational need in a school or an issue about appropriate staffing and resourcing levels, in the context of delivering the National Curriculum and the integration of children with special educational needs.

School-based behaviour of excluded children

The school-based behaviours reported to have led to a child's exclusion were obtained from three main sources: from information on file in the education department; from interviews with head and class teachers (almost always held separately); and from behaviour rating scales. They were thus reported behaviours, rather than observed behaviours. Schools in LEA 1 were encouraged to inform the LEA about the reasons for exclusion using standardized forms or letters, which varied according to the division of the LEA. These forms/letters did not have a precoded list of possible behaviours as did LEA 2. However, schools did not always use these standardized methods of reporting to the LEA, or indeed supply all the information requested. Information on file, in the form of letters to parents and the LEA were followed through and cross-referenced with reasons given for the exclusion at interview. It soon became obvious that there was rarely a single or even main reason for most exclusions, although there was a precipitating event. In other words most exclusions were the result of a protracted period of difficulty in school with and for a particular child, with a particular event triggering an exclusion. Letters from schools to parents and the LEA did not always specify the behaviour(s) which were the reason for an exclusion: they used general descriptions such as 'uncontrollable', 'unacceptable', 'aggressive' or 'anti-social'.

Physical aggression

Physical aggression was a significant issue in about three-quarters of the cases, and although this was more often directed at other children, in nearly a third of the case studies it involved staff too. However, it would seem that some of this aggression towards staff was the result of staff intervention in a situation, such as an attempt to prevent the further attack of another child, that is the aggression did not generally start as aggression towards staff. In only a handful of cases was this aggression described as simply 'fighting' with other children. In all of the cases where the physical aggression amounted to fighting another child only, a fixed term exclusion was given. Events needed to be much more serious and prolonged before schools resorted to longer periods of exclusion.

For example Pippa had been having great difficulties with her peers in school for over a year before she was permanently excluded. Her head teacher said of the situation: 'There wasn't a lunchtime or playtime went by without Pippa hitting or kicking someone.'

Tommy was excluded from an EBD special school which felt they did not have the expertise to help him. It was the level of physical aggression in the end which led to his permanent exclusion, according to his class teacher:

He was capable of achieving great damage. He wasn't a coordinated child and when he did lose his temper his control over his own actions became far less . . . once his teeth were sunk in he would do a lot of damage. Only when some child or adult got too close he would bite, and throw things, he did do a lot of throwing.

Shane was described as generally disruptive and disobedient, but it was the physical aggression which caused most concern to his class and head teacher. His class teacher described two such events:

There was something wild about his behaviour . . . he picked up these mathematical cubes and threw them in her [another child] face . . . he didn't look even particularly angry or upset. There was a feeling just of casual violence . . . it was these kinds of incidents that were dangerous for other children . . . on a field trip he got a flagpole with a pointed end and was throwing it like a javelin at other people and damned close too, he carried on after he'd been asked to stop.

Shane's indefinite exclusion came at the end of a week-long residential trip when the site organizers wrote to the school complaining about the child's behaviour. This indefinite exclusion was made permanent.

Some children were excluded for fixed term periods for fighting other children, as this was explicitly against the school's behaviour policy or code of conduct. However, even these events tended to come after a period of concern about other aspects of the child's behaviour: often this amounted to general disruptiveness, sometimes allegations about bullying other children were made. For example, Daniel's head teacher said of him: 'He has an image to keep up . . . He wants to be seen to be tough. He's devious, he's fast becoming a thug really . . . he's involved in bullying.'

Henry had already had a permanent exclusion from another school when we investigated the outcome of an indefinite exclusion from his next school. Although the physical aggression was relatively minor in this case, it was these behaviours that other children and parents were complaining about. His head teacher described him thus:

> He's incredibly powerful, he's encouraged by mum . . . He sets his own agenda. He decides what he wants to do and where he wants to do it. He takes up the teachers' time, my time, supervisors' time, disproportionately. Children complain about him, he knocks them and digs them when they go past. It's all attention seeking, trying to form relationships with other people. Parents have taken their children away from the school because of Henry . . . He's actually fairly bright but underattaining. Even with 25 hours SNA he's difficult to contain. He insults other people's families, swears a lot, lies, throws things in class.

Some children were viewed more sympathetically despite their potential for physical aggression towards other children. Their behaviour was viewed as to do with an inability to control their temper, rather than a wish to hurt other people. Dale, for example, was given a fixed term exclusion for throwing a cricket ball in another child's face, but he was not seen as a serious threat to other children's safety. Bob had been permanently excluded from two other primary schools and other children were described as frightened of him, yet his class teacher was able to say of him: 'He really does not want to be naughty . . . he knows he needs help with his temper . . . but I can see how he has got to where he is now.' Bob's teacher was of the opinion that although his primary school could probably 'contain' him, he needed additional help over and above what she felt able to provide, if he was going to be able to stay in mainstream schooling as he got older.

High level disruption

Instances of physical aggression did not always involve disruption which affected the whole school, although some of the individuals referred to in the previous subsection were involved in events affecting much bigger groups of children, often the running of the whole school. Many of these situations involved absconding from the school site. For example, Pippa absconded from the school site 'countless times' and regularly left the class-room. Often her class teacher had to leave the rest of the class to be super-vised by the teacher of the children in the next classroom, while he went to calm her down. This meant leaving nearly 60 children to the supervision of one teacher. The school governors began to query why so many chil-dren were having their education disrupted, and after one particularly high profile event she was eventually permanently excluded.

Nathan's behaviour in the classroom was described by his teacher in the following way: 'Uncontrollable lashing out, shaking head, no eye contact. When you have 30 children in the class and a child is throwing a table at you there is not a lot you can do . . . you have to think of the other 30 children, they were petrified of him.'

Catherine was viewed as 'out of control' at times by her head teacher:

She would run very easily and when she ran you had no guarantee of finding her . . . We had to remove her from the classroom [at times] and I would have a seat for her in my office and she would start screaming and shouting . . . sometimes she wouldn't just go verbally out of control but physically as well . . . she was a very strong girl. I would say she was out of control in these situations . . . I don't think she was aware of what she was doing by any means . . . I have had a couple of occasions where I have had to hold her on the floor because she was so out of control and there I had to stay until I could get assistance . . . normally from the social services department.

Gerald's behaviour was described as escalating to a situation where the school could not 'contain' him:

He would swear, the swearing was a main part of it at first . . . he would swear at anybody and everybody. We had an SNA working with him and he would just swear all day at her. He then became a lot more violent, hitting other children . . . running out of the class . . . refusing to do the work . . . [he] just began to behave in a way we couldn't contain in the normal classroom environment.

In a minority of cases, children's behaviour became so uncontrollable, in the view of the teachers interviewed, that they felt they had to try and restrain the child. This was a particularly worrying issue for these teachers, because they did not have any training in the use of restraint or holding techniques. At most, some individuals in a school might have read some written guidelines, but there was clearly a major gap between this and put-ting what they had read into practice. The head teacher of a junior school, which derived its pupils from a large local authority housing estate, des-cribed a playground fight which was viewed as potentially so serious that the staff present tried to restrain the child: 'Staff got themselves into a situation which they shouldn't have, by physically lifting him up and bring-ing him in . . . they didn't know what to do, this sort of thing just doesn't happen.' In the opinion of the head teacher, the staff may have been found guilty of assault in their handling of him. In other such situations several staff had difficulty in restraining children, through lack of understanding about and experience in using such procedures.

Nearly half of the children were literally difficult to contain in the classroom: they would run out and around the school, and most of these children would run away from the school premises too, on occasion. For example, Gareth would not only run around his own junior school but the neighbouring infant school as well. Schools often felt unable to guarantee the safety of a child, as in the case of Catherine: 'It came to a point where just sending her out at playtimes was problematic, her running was planned, she rarely ran out of temper . . . We could no longer guarantee her safety, we had no way of containing her.'

Disturbed behaviour?

In about a third of the cases teachers described children as 'disturbed' more than disruptive, such descriptions were almost always associated with intimations that the child was beyond their experience and needed some kind of specialist help. Such children were viewed as very unsettling to other children, in a way which went beyond even some of the high level disruptions. On an everyday level, for example, teachers described how other children would flinch when such a child passed or would not want to go to the book corner if the child was there. Class teachers would usually emphasize just how different they felt such children were. They tended to stress the length of their teaching experience, but their lack of experience in teaching such children. Bradley's class teacher said: 'In 30 years of teaching I have never met a child like him . . . I wasn't really prepared for what he was like . . . one moment he was good the next he was up on the table screaming, hitting other children . . . there was no indication, you couldn't anticipate what he would do.'

There tended to be agreement between class and head teachers about the nature of such children, as the case of Thomas illustrates. His class teacher described the way he presented:

> There was no escalation of the problem, it was presented on day one. On the first morning he exhibited a full blown temper tantrum which was followed by Thomas placing himself in the school cloakroom, curled up and in the view of the class teacher . . . in a foetal position . . . He was terribly unhappy, but he just wouldn't tell anybody why or what was wrong.

His head teacher said of him:

> I feel he's got such a deep-seated problem, I don't know how to deal with it. He needs help and that's my opinion as a teacher. I've been teaching for 31 years and I've never come across one like that before. We've had naughty boys who are uncooperative and had to take all sorts of measures, but no one like that.

Yet class and head teachers did not always agree about whether such a child should be excluded. Thomas's class teacher was surprised and upset when he was permanently excluded for a high profile event at lunchtime, which had involved the intervention of the head teacher. However, the head teacher was of the opinion that he should not be in a mainstream school and would only get help if he was permanently excluded.

A similar story is shown in Tommy's permanent exclusion from a special school:

> *Class teacher*: 'Sadly I really did like Tommy, the sense of failure I felt . . .' [became tearful]
> *Deputy head teacher* [acting head teacher at the time]: 'You were devastated by it, you didn't want me to do it.'
> *Class teacher*: 'But in the end I knew this child was so disturbed and had such an awful, awful life . . .'

Mainstream teachers tended to assume that there were people with expertise in other professions and facilities who were better equipped to help these children. However, special school staff also voiced similar opinions. For example, the head teacher of a special school for children with emotional and behavioural difficulties (a psychologist by training) said:

> If an adult behaved in the way that some of these children do, they would be sectioned . . . I think we have got children here who are actually ill . . . We are not just talking about conduct-disordered children who are naughty. It seems that by definition there should have been clinical psychologist and psychiatric support . . . I think we are battling, as more children are in mainstream, with the very extreme end of the continuum. Fewer and fewer children are being sent out of county [to therapeutic environments/residential facilities].

Other concerns

In several cases teachers mentioned that they felt the physical size of a child had a bearing on both how the child's behaviour was perceived by teachers, as well as its impact on other children. For example, Jordon was very large for his age and attended a school with very little outside space, off a main high street in central London. At home he lived in a one-bedroomed flat with no garden. His head teacher believed the school was simply not spacious enough for him, but also that he had not learned how to play appropriately with other children:

> He is clumsy and knocks over other children . . . He's not particularly spiteful . . . He's just large and has difficulty controlling himself. There's a lot of rough and tumble with his mother's older brothers . . . he does play roughly and tends to 'play' with adults outside of school. If he has hurt them, they may not have said. So when he starts wrestling with children of his own age in school, he just doesn't realize his own

strength . . . He's actually got no idea how to play with his peer group, he never has had, we've talked to the mother. From reception onwards, it has always been the same . . . he really doesn't know his own strength. I've lost three little girls because of him, their parents have taken them away because of him.

A minority of the children were viewed as displaying inappropriate sexualized behaviour. Two of the girls were described as sexually precocious: this caused concern both for male staff but also for the girls' safety. In one case a girl who had been resident during the week in accommodation attached to her EBD school was asked to attend school on a daily basis instead. Three of the boys were viewed as sexually threatening to girls: one boy made 'obscene' comments to them; another exposed himself to other children (and adults too on occasion); in the third case, the boy sexually assaulted a little girl. Although all these events might be viewed as highly emotive, these behaviours were always only part of a range of behaviours they were displaying at school. A minority of children tried to hurt themselves or engaged in activities considered dangerous to themselves while in school: for example, cutting themselves or banging their heads, running into the road or hanging out of an upper storey window.

Despite numerous difficulties many class teachers, as already illustrated, showed affection for many of these children, as well as some insight into the possible origins of their problems. For example Nathan's head teacher described him as 'A boy full of anger, yet full of charm . . . I wanted to cuddle him . . . he needed to cry. He needed a crisis to bring him through.' Daniel's head teacher said of him: 'Daniel like all children has a super side to him. I believe it's his background and circumstances . . . He can show a very caring side.'

Many of the children were described as relatively isolated, with other children often being wary of them. It was clear to many teachers that some of these children did not have the social skills to form positive friendships and that they were especially vulnerable in the less structured parts of the day. Children were often described as lacking in self-confidence and as having low self-esteem.

Behaviour management and discipline in the schools

The majority of the schools visited were in the process of further developing behaviour management and discipline policies, which were described in a range of ways, such as codes of conduct and charters . The most common packages mentioned were the 'Assertive Discipline' (Canter and Canter 1992) and 'Circle Time' (Mosley 1993) approaches, although most schools adapted and added to these ideas. The enthusiasm was noticeable among head teachers who had recently adopted one of these approaches. If an approach had been adopted wholeheartedly by staff they generally reported that it had an immediate impact in terms of improving staff morale and children's behaviour. However, as some head teachers pointed out, there was a need to keep developing new ideas about tackling issues of behaviour and discipline, in order to keep the momentum going in a school.

Most schools were enthusiastic about involving children in developing the rules or charter. As one head teacher commented on how the children were involved in developing a charter about how they should behave, 'Children are very good at this, they know what they should do . . . it doesn't mean they always do it.'

Some schools had schools councils which were used as a vehicle to help develop and agree policies. For example, in one of the London schools each of the classes had two representatives, who met with the head teacher and deputy for half an hour once a week on a Friday to report back and discuss issues which had arisen in their classes during the week.

However, contact with and support from parents about behaviour and discipline was varied. There were numerous reasons for this. Sometimes it was to do with lack of time on the part of school staff to undertake any meaningful consultation; often there was insufficient support from parents for such consultations, that is they did not attend the consultative meetings organized.

In some such schools teachers talked of great difficulties with parents in relation to what is appropriate (even legally allowable) behaviour management and discipline in a school. One head teacher held a number of consultative meetings with parents during the course of developing their behaviour management and discipline policy. She said of this process: 'A lot of the parents thought that the children should be stood out in front of everybody when they are naughty . . . A lot of parents wanted to give personal permission to smack their child . . . A lot of parents think a man will make a difference [to discipline].'

Such consultations were viewed as useful in terms of parent education and in developing support for the schools policy, but they took time at the end of the working day, and in that sense could be viewed as an addition to existing workloads. However, most schools realized that there was important potential in enlisting the support of parents in these areas, as well as providing them with more support in the management of their children at home, but many felt that this could not easily be done within the resources available. One school was paying for a consultant to come in and work with parents about behaviour management and discipline in the home. This programme was complementary to the schools system. Most head teachers reported that parents regularly approached them for advice about managing the behaviour and discipline of their children at home.

Schools were divided about whether they wanted internal or outside support with behaviour. In the London borough, schools could expect to gain access to a behaviour support service for about two sessions a week for one term, in a school year. Members of this team would work with individuals, groups or whole classes. Some head teachers were very clear in their view that staff needed outside support with behaviour management; as one head teacher said:

> I think you need somebody from outside. Teachers often get too emotionally involved in the whole thing . . . People from the outside come in fresh. It never seems to quite work internally because everybody has got their own problems, everybody has got too much to do. When you've got somebody from outside coming in to help it can be wonderful . . . some individuals [named individual in service] are very, very high calibre.

On the other hand, another head teacher in the same borough decided to appoint a half time teacher (a former deputy head) to support staff in a range of practical ways. She felt that sometimes the needs of some class teachers were too pressing to wait for their allocation of time with the behaviour support team, which could be one or two terms away:

> I've got some new teachers to the school for whom the challenges that these children present are very new to them and they'll find it an uphill struggle. With the best will in the world, it's a huge shock to the system to meet children who will challenge them [when they] don't have strategies because they haven't had the experience to develop them. So, I haven't got time to let them evolve those strategies. I need to get someone in there to say look, this will work.

A concern for all schools was the behaviour of a relatively small minority of children. It was acknowledged by most of these teachers that some children did not know how to behave appropriately and in effect had to be taught to behave appropriately in school. The extent to which whole-school behaviour policies can contribute to this social learning is debatable. Whole-school behaviour management strategies like 'Assertive Discipline' and 'Circle Time' acknowledge that there will be children who will not respond to these structures, or even the individual programmes constructed for them within mainstream education. It was the degree of challenge presented by the child who got excluded, usually coupled with a perception of lack of support from the child's parent or carer, which tended to render behaviour and discipline policies ineffective in dealing with some individuals. These difficulties could be compounded for some of the children who spent periods of time accommodated by the local authority.

School–home relationship and communication

Nearly half of the excluded children were accommodated by the local authority, just before, during or after the period(s) of exclusion, as has already been indicated. Thus school – home contact was very problematic in terms of who the school should actually liaise with. In addition another seven children had either major social services involvement and/or disruption in their lives which involved moving residence between birth parents. In all, nearly two-thirds of the children were not living in a consistent family home during the period under investigation. Schools of course were only too well aware of this disruption but were not always kept up to date with the details.

Andy, for example, spent less than a term in a mainstream junior school, after being transferred from an EBD special unit. There were no meetings between staff at the unit and the mainstream school, and the head teacher did not meet the child's mother before Andy was transferred to the custody of his father on the other side of the city. The child used to arrive at school in a social services taxi at 8.15 in the morning. Apparently the social services department did not check with the school to find out whether there would be staff on site to look after him at this time of day. In this situation there was little possibility of home and school working together. The head teacher described how there was no contact between either Andy's parents and the school, or his special unit and the school before he arrived in the school: 'Everybody needed to cooperate if it was going to be a success. The mother needed to come into the school and so on . . . All that was just left, from the annual review [in his special unit] and the phone call asking whether I'd take him, then he arrived on the doorstep.'

Another head teacher made a similar point about the difficulty of involving some parents: 'Involving parents may be preventive but exclusion often comes about because parents are unwilling to be involved.'

In other cases the school had spent a great deal of time with the parents before a child was excluded, but sometimes this was recognized as not enough to support some parents, as Gary's head teacher explains:

The parents were very supportive in terms of wanting to help . . . mum in particular. I always got on with mum ever since Gareth had been in school. She has always been involved and listens to what we have to say and attempts to put it into practice. But I don't feel she actually understood the strategies or was prepared to carry them through.

However, as we saw in the last chapter, parents did not always welcome being contacted by the school: 'Some parents do not like being told that their children are constantly in trouble. When we say, well you should know what is happening, some say "Well, it's your problem to sort out in school." Some dread the phone ringing.'

Some teachers showed recognition and understanding of the difficulties for parents in this situation. Jordon's head teacher said of his mother:

It's hard to hear what bad or unhappy things, or uncomfortable things your child is doing . . . she has tried to deflect. Sometimes she avoids coming into school but on other occasions when I do engage with her, she wants to discuss the situation, but I feel sometimes that it's very hard for her . . . The more we've been able to say positive things the more we've been more comfortable, obviously . . . I think she's beginning to feel that we don't also blame her.

Parents often started out trying to support the school in trying to modify their child's behaviour. However, if they were unable to effect any change, the situation could begin to deteriorate:

> Most parents are very supportive, including Mr O'Leary . . . they'd [father and/or stepmother] come and get him, or sometimes he'd be kept at home when he was difficult. It worked for two terms. Then it started going downhill, several teachers complained about him. We lost the support of his father . . . [head teacher became tearful at this point] Mr O'Leary feels I've let him down.

As the last quote indicates, this lack of success could be taken very badly by some teachers. Other schools were of the opinion that it was up to parents to agree with them and do what the school expected. For example the head teacher of an oversubscribed suburban voluntary aided school said in relation to his expectations of parents: 'Parents are asked to fill in a form agreeing to the school behaviour policy. Like a contract really . . .'

After a serious incident which is likely to result in an exclusion one head teacher said: 'I always take the child home. On the doorstep or if I am invited in I can sit down and say, "Look, this is the score", almost without exception I am received with courtesy, respect, friendship and support. I think these are very profitable visits.' Although in relation to consulting parents about the development of behaviour and discipline policy the same head teacher said: 'I don't consult with parents. I take the old-fashioned approach that I'm in charge. Although I claim to be a progressive. I'm in charge and that's the way it is . . . I don't browbeat children, if a child wants to speak to me, I will shut the door and they can say what they like.'

Regular contact with parents and carers was more difficult, if not impossible, in special schools because the children tended to come from a wide geographical area. Many children arrived by bus or taxi, which in London could involve several boroughs. Thus incidental contact with parents dropping off or collecting children at school was lost, and any special meetings called could involve some travel and thus expense for parents who were usually relatively impoverished.

Other agencies: liaison and support

Most schools were aware that other agencies were involved with a family, although they were often not kept up to date with what was going on, such as where the child was living and what interventions (if any) were being tried with a family or child. Teachers recognized the issue about confidentiality, but were concerned that they could be offering inappropriate and/or conflicting advice to some families. One head teacher suggested a termly list from social services offices informing schools of which families/ children they are involved with, with a contact person for teachers who had major concerns about an individual. He said of the current situation:

Many times I have been concerned about children, only to find that social services are working with them. They are not obliged to tell us . . . So, here I am suggesting an EWO goes round, or the EP sees them when already somebody has recognized a need in the child and is trying to help him. Extra help might not be what they need when the first lot isn't finished yet . . . [they may get] . . . different messages. Social services are very obliging when they come round, [but] I do feel a need to make things better, communications-wise. It would be nice if there was a statutory obligation to report to schools, we need to time giving help properly. Sometimes we are going in with the full army of support services, it can seem like overkill.

In relation to social services departments the common criticism was the lack of information passed on to the school, as well as the tendency not to keep the school up to date about moves in residence and other details. There was a recognition in some schools that this may relate to time and resource pressures in social services departments. However, there was anger at the lack of proper consultation and follow-up in cases where the school had raised child protection concerns. When teachers were showing concern about a child who was in their care for over 30 hours a week, they could not understand the apparent lack of urgency in other agencies in relation to children who seemed, to them, so unusual and in need.

Some schools had managed to establish beneficial working relationships with social services: 'We work quite closely with the family resource centre, or we have done up until now . . . We worked on a weekly basis, with John coming in until very recently. That's all changed because they are restructuring . . . we really valued their help.'

Teachers with long experience of working in London said they could remember more support and multi-agency working. They often reported feeling lacking in support and believed that despite the talk about 'working together', all of the trends were in the opposite direction.

In terms of education support services, this was a case in point. Most primary schools had at most two half days of educational psychologist time per school term. This was barely enough time to deal with the children causing most concern, let alone begin to engage in more preventive work with children who were beginning to cause concern in school. As one long-serving head teacher of a large (560 children) junior school said: 'I'd like more EP time, two half days a term is no time at all . . . There was a time you could just get on the phone and ask for some help . . . I've got less than ten children who are what you'd call "hard core problems" . . . Let's face it, they take up so much of our time, especially with the need to involve other services.'

Shamus had already had two fixed term exclusions by the time the educational psychologist had time to observe him:

Shamus has only recently seen an EP . . . all we have had is informal chats. It's only recently that he has been formally assessed because there are so many other children that they keep being dropped off the list. This is not unusual, there is a great long list and we only have so much resources, so those on the borderline never get the help they need. [Shamus was assessed as outside the group of children who should go forward for a statement.]

Other teachers made the point that an individual educational psychologist was not always very useful or expert in offering support and advice about behaviour problems. In this respect a school could feel very much on their own:

Educational psychology support depends very much on the individual EP. Some have particular expertise and some excellent strategies for dealing with behaviour problems, others are more geared towards learning difficulties and assessment. Our EP . . . the main use is identifying children with learning difficulties, she hasn't been much help in the way of offering strategies for dealing with behavioural problems.

On the other hand, some schools were very positive about the quality of the support they were getting, but felt that they simply did not get the time they needed: 'We've a superb relationship with our EP but he just hasn't got the time.'

Schools tried to enlist the support of a range of agencies, as indeed they are expected to do under the new Code of Practice in relation to special educational needs. However, this depended upon the willingness of families to see other professionals. Thomas's head teacher said:

The previous school had set up a programme of child and family guidance . . . [the] father knocked that on the head pretty quickly. So, they [the parents] paid privately to see a psychiatrist . . . she [the psychiatrist] did ring me when all this blew up [the permanent exclusion] to say that she was not going to put it in writing [but that] . . . she would not be surprised if there wasn't some sort of abuse.

Many teachers reported increasing difficulties in enlisting the support of other agencies:

the way things are going everybody is becoming more isolated. We had good links with child and family therapy, they are a new trust . . . we couldn't even have it if we paid for it. At a time when we feel we want to be networking we are actually more isolated. It just seems ridiculous to me, it's a way they can reach all children, if they were to work in schools. Instead they rely on families taking them there and many times families just don't go.

Indeed the child and family guidance service stopped all direct referrals from schools for a period during the period of research in LEA 1, advising that all referrals must come via a GP.

In one of the London boroughs, where the child and family guidance service was part-funded by the education department, some clinics were held at certain schools on a monthly basis and weekly at accessible community facilities. However, this service was threatened with cuts from the education department during the period of research. Schools in receipt of this service were glad to have some additional support to offer families:

> It's much better since they've been based at [local clinic] as well as [main centre] . . . I've referred people to the main clinic before and they just didn't go, because it's a long way on public transport and because it's in the middle of a big estate . . . Now it's at their local clinic, where they go for their hearing checks and so on, it's more theirs . . . We've got about four families attending now.

Another head teacher described how useful the service was: 'The child guidance have a clinic, a surgery, they call it a drop-in for parents in this school. So I send a letter home to parents saying, if you've got any concerns about your children's behaviour let us know at the school and we'll arrange a meeting.'

Some schools were keen to get the advice from other specialists, but sometimes found it could be difficult to implement their ideas within the confines of a school. The head teacher of Wayne and Andrew said: 'We all went to speak to a play therapist who suggested that we allow the kids space to play, seeing as they had massive problems. The problem with this was that if they could play for part of the day they couldn't see why they shouldn't play for the whole day.'

Several head teachers looked somewhat blank when the issue of support from other agencies was raised. They reported feeling very much alone and left to deal with whatever problems a child or family presented to the school. One head teacher found similar problems with agencies outside the school generally: 'They're not talking to each other and they're certainly not talking to us. Since the child comes to our school every day, you'd think we'd be the hub of the universe in terms of information exchange . . . but we're not getting anything at all. I don't think that's very helpful.'

The lack of appropriate support for some children in school is illustrated by the comment made by a visiting clinical psychologist to the head teacher of an EBD school: 'You are running a day unit here really, without the staff.' In other words, the clinical psychologist was suggesting that a number of the children had mental health problems but were being cared for by teachers.

Why children were excluded: head teachers' accounts

As has already been established, the responsibility for an exclusion rests with the head teacher. Head teachers emphasized that the excluded child had been of some concern prior to the exclusion and usually it was either an accumulation of incidents or a particularly high profile event which precipitated an exclusion. Shamus's fixed term exclusion was given for fighting, but in reality,

> The actual incident was an accumulation of behaviour that just wasn't changing . . . it was a case where we could deal with it so many times and use all the sanctions like playtime detentions and so on. With children like Shamus they need to get out and run around and do something with their aggression. If they have been sitting in the hall quietly then they come up to the classroom wound up . . . he was almost constantly in that situation.

Bob's head teacher gave him a fixed term exclusion for tripping up a teacher in the playground. He said of the behaviour which came before this event: 'There was a challenge going on and we kept threatening . . . He needed to understand that when he's heading for an exclusion we mean it. We put up with a lot of kickings, pushings and shovings, just general aggressiveness, bullying and anti-social behaviour.'

It was often in the less structured parts of the day that problems could occur. This also meant that any outburst could be witnessed by most of the school. In the case of Levi, four members of staff were involved in an event which led to a fixed term exclusion:

> Levi was lashing out as he came in for dinner. He was observed to be in a very bad mood. He ended up having a complete temper tantrum, rolling on the floor and hitting other children. He refused to move, so four members of staff had to remove him . . . It was such a muddle, when you have to go through something like that, it was an absolute nightmare . . . it took at least a good three-quarters of an hour to calm him down.

In the case of Paul, the event leading to his permanent exclusion came after a long period of difficulty, as well as consultation with his parents. The final event happened in front of the whole school at the end of the school year:

> Nothing could have prevented that exclusion. I've half-killed myself. My staff were chivvied into half-killing themselves . . . The severity of the incident was such that after all the work we'd put in, the head teacher and deputy head teacher were physically abused in front of 250 children and then Paul went off shouting around the whole school.

In Pippa's case, the precipitating event came when she was brought to school unwillingly by new foster parents on a day when the head teacher was not on site:

> Pippa wouldn't go into the school properly or go to the classroom. What followed was a horrendous three hours, in which she was running up and down the room, sweeping papers off the desk and picking up things. She was shouting, swearing, pacing, sweeping papers

off the desk . . . she started kicking things, she kicked a hole in the door . . . Her mood was up and down, at times she was curled up in a chair.

Occasionally incidents occurred in class and were perceived to be unpredictable: 'It was totally out of the blue, this particular incident. There was nothing we could have done to prevent it. He just got up in the middle of the class and hit another child over the head . . . all the children know they will be excluded for an unprovoked attack on another child.'

It was clear that some head teachers thought that the children they had excluded were misplaced in mainstream education. There was also frustration about a perceived lack of options. Resources were a key issue though, in that some teachers also felt that almost all children could be coped with, given enough staff with appropriate training. Resources related primarily to physical space and staff, especially appropriately trained and experienced staff. The gap between pleading for a few hours NTA support for a child in mainstream school and special provision was all too apparent to some teachers. Some head teachers felt they had been 'tricked' into taking a particular child, who really needed special educational provision. For example, Chris's head teacher said:

It wouldn't be unprofessional to say that we were tricked into taking him. He shouldn't have been placed with us. We only got half the picture. We only got the positive part of the picture . . . He wasn't ready to work in a classroom. In his previous school he was in a special unit. He opted where he was going to work, in a very small group or in the classroom. Most of the time he was one-to-one with an NTA. They had a quiet room and a safe room. The only option here is with me . . . What makes me bitter is that we had to resort to exclusion to get him into a special school.

Pippa's head teacher offered the view that she was in need of a special school placement, a view shared by her mother and social worker: 'I really don't think that she is able to work in a mainstream school, with lots of people around her. There could have been many occasions where the child could have been excluded. The event . . . was very high profile and right at the beginning of the school year.' However, Pippa was out of school for a whole year before she was found a place at an EBD special school.

Even when teachers believed the child to be misplaced in mainstream education they tended to feel they should have been able to do more for the child: 'I feel bad about it, because in a way I feel we failed him, but he definitely needs small numbers, which was not in our budget . . . the statement only provided two hours support a day.' This quote also reveals the resource aspect to the whole situation.

However, a special school placement was not always a long-term solution, as Tommy's case illustrates: 'I don't think there was any more we could have done for Tommy. We actually went out on a limb for him. We maintained his presence here longer than was reasonable.' (Tommy was attending an EBD special day school.) Tommy was believed to be in need of a residential therapeutic environment, by both his teacher and social worker.

Several teachers mentioned feeling that there was a lack of options in dealing with the most difficult behaviour:

> I feel within the school there is a lack of serious disciplinary measures at my disposal, where you have got behaviour that isn't morally bad but is so extreme that it's significantly getting in the way of other children learning. You are not being fair to the other children and I've got some really keen children whose learning is affected because of the behaviour of some of the class . . . and I have very few measures that I can take . . . Internal exclusion, that is what you need . . . You resource that group adequately and then they can be reintroduced to the main class when appropriate.

Some teachers believed that there was a conflict between the way they were both expected to discipline children as well as counsel them: '[There's] too much discussion around why they think they have done it, how they think they could do better. I think there is a line, a boundary and when you cross it the sanction comes in. The kids need signposts but once they cross it, that is it.'

Several teachers pointed to the gap in disciplinary measures left by corporal punishment, while quickly saying they did not agree with it personally in the great majority of cases. One teacher pointed out that 'At one time the worst that could happen to a child was corporal punishment.' This teacher recalled an incident in his early school career, where a child had set fire to the waste paper bin and was caned. He was in no doubt that such a child would now be excluded from school, perhaps even permanently, depending upon the behaviour which preceded this event.

Lack of space was often mentioned as a factor, both in terms of classrooms, playgrounds and for providing space for children to 'cool off' and thus avert a crisis. In some schools the issue of space was acute. For example, one middle school was in temporary huts because the school building had 'concrete cancer': 'In this accommodation [i.e. huts] there is nowhere for a child to go to calm down. Kevin didn't like being in the hut . . . Well, a lot of children don't like it, you can't walk to the toilet, it's in a corner of the room. There's no corridor.'

Some teachers believed a withdrawal facility (which were fairly common in secondary schools in the 1970s) would prevent exclusions: 'I've never had a child who was so defiant . . . Someone like Ian needs isolation. The ideal to me would be a room where he couldn't get out, but where he was supervised to do some work for a short period, a cooling-off period, time out but controlled. This school doesn't lend itself physically to that approach.' Another teacher said: 'If the government really wants us to keep these children in mainstream school and I think they should be, almost all. In my experience most of these children could be managed in school if we had the internal resources, two members of staff to provide internal exclusion, programmes of work.'

However, one school had experimented unsuccessfully with setting up such a facility on site:

> We decided to set up our own unit. We had three children who couldn't be contained in the class. We took them out, but in fact there wasn't enough [children]. We were trying to set up a unit over a holiday with no additional money. The LEA unit was set up over a term with thousands of pounds. The principle is great [i.e. units] but you need people with the right skills and funding. However, it also meant that other children suffered, all my resources went into that. I didn't have enough to spread around the school.

As with the various forms of withdrawal, isolation or internal exclusion, many of the other suggestions had resource implications. Smaller classes and extra staff were mentioned frequently: 'All these children need is positive rewards and care and attention . . . One extra member of staff in the lower school would give us that.' Another teacher made a similar point:

> If we had smaller classes it would be easier to cope with the children we do have, a high proportion need extra help and input . . . when some are away and you're down to say 25 or 26 children, you can really see the difference. Also, I think a full-time NTA as support and it should be consistent NTA support, so that the children get to know them . . . When these children work on a one-to-one with an NTA they develop a really good relationship, you really get to know the child in this situation.

Sometimes teachers were frustrated by events which seemed to suggest that the child only attracted extra resources for support after they had been permanently excluded from school: 'The educational psychologist felt he shouldn't go into mainstream, without 15 hours support. Had we had 15 hours support, we might have been able to contain him.'

The experience of excluding a primary age child from school: head teachers' accounts

Official primary school exclusions are relatively rare, particularly the permanent category. Most head teachers we spoke to had very little experience of having to resort to them. It was clear that the experience of having to go to a permanent exclusion was often traumatic for staff. The feeling of personal failure, as we have already seen, was frequently expressed. However, there was also the intimation that they had learned how to go through the process properly and would resort to it again if need be. A clear distinction was made between a fixed term exclusion as a useful disciplinary sanction and a permanent exclusion as a last resort.

Many schools viewed even fixed term exclusions as very rare events. For example a head teacher of an urban school said, referring to the fourth fixed term exclusion she had given in 12 years as a head teacher, 'It's not something I would want to use . . . generally it is a very negative experience for all concerned. It is known that if a child attacks or is seen to attack another adult in the school then he/she knows that that means exclusion. Every exclusion that I have done has been for that reason.'

Another head teacher who had permanently excluded three children in six years said: 'We don't talk about exclusion, you don't like to admit it, you feel a failure. You keep thinking was there anything else I could have done? You want to do right by the child.' This teacher was of the opinion that in her experience a permanent exclusion related to a child in need of a special school place. All of the three children that she had permanently excluded had been given a special school place after the exclusion. She spoke of the trauma of the first permanent exclusion she felt she had to do, but said that she had since learned how to go through the process more efficiently, when she and her staff believed it to be necessary. Some head teachers had never resorted to a permanent exclusion before the one under investigation: 'Chris was the first child I'd had to do it with. I agonized for a whole day before I did it. I knew, knowing all of the situation Chris was in, that I was doing exactly what everyone else had done to him in school and elsewhere. We wanted him to be happy at school and be with all of us. I felt let down by the lack of support I was getting.' Yet she went on to say:

> It's [exclusion] something that more generally we [i.e. head teachers] are resorting to . . . Having agonized and done it once, it never seems quite so bad. You begin to think, why should I put up with that . . . I don't like doing it, but I've done it three times this year now for different children. Some children are excluded at lunchtimes as they are such a liability.

Many head teachers wanted to emphasize that the process towards a permanent exclusion was a difficult one and was a decision by no means lightly taken: 'In my experience these children are very unusual cases. Most heads will do anything to avoid exclusion. The path to exclusion is very, very difficult. The worst thing of all is coping with the guilt of the staff, who feel they have failed.'

Some head teachers had experienced an appeal against the school from the LEA: 'We have permanently excluded one child from here, it went to appeal. In the course of the appeal it was counted up that we had tried 28 different strategies to help that child. We felt that we'd done more than our fair share.' Such events were extremely difficult for schools to come to terms with, especially if the child was reinstated in the school; the head teacher was usually very concerned about the message that such a decision would give to other children in the school, in relation to appropriate behaviour and disciplinary sanctions.

The point was made numerous times that exclusion serves to draw attention to a child's needs, both for the parents and the LEA:

I think exclusion serves a purpose to draw attention to the child, the school, the parents that something serious is going on, that all concerned need to take stock. I don't think excluding a child for a day . . . it may be just a day off, that's not an exclusion that's working . . . I would use it as a warning, after a series of things. Exclusion can safeguard others, but all you're doing is pushing the problem somewhere else.

In particular head teachers wanted to get parents to take more responsibility for their children's behaviour: 'It's the only thing in some cases which makes the parents take note because we're actually impinging on their life . . . It tends to be parents who don't support what's going on, who pay lip service to what we do. They give us an agreement . . . but if they have got to look after them, they'll take notice.'

Exclusion was seen as a way of 'drawing the line' in relation to appropriate behaviour in a school and was considered as essential in keeping order by some head teachers:

I don't think that exclusion in terms of helping the child is useful . . . but it does underline what is said goes. There has to be a point where you say 'What you are doing is so bad, so disgusting, so anti-social that I will remove you from the school.' . . . There is a point where you feel 'I don't care about you, I care more about all the other children.' Exclusion is a failure on the school . . . [But] we have them for five and a half hours a day, we can't change everything! Parents' attitudes have a greater influence than we can have.

Thus exclusion was not generally seen as immediately useful to the individual in any specific way. Sometimes an exclusion ultimately did lead to other resources to help the child:

They're [exclusions] not that useful really. In the last exclusion we had three case conferences, we tried to get a social worker attached to the child and nothing had been done . . . So, when he brings in a knife and threatens other people, an exclusion followed. Actually the threat of an exclusion or an exclusion can get the ball rolling . . . his two exclusions got him the support he should have had before.

The National Curriculum was cited by some interviewees in explaining the pressures which created an environment in which exclusions were likely to occur:

We are delivering the National Curriculum, but at a price. We need facilities for children like these – if they provided the appropriate facilities for these children, then the chances are that these children will achieve, so that the chances are you will have less frustrated children and adults in the future. They must deal with the problem now. Nathan didn't want his peer group to know of his lack of achievement, at 12 not being able to read and write well.

These pressures were also felt in special schools:

> Back in the 1970s when you came to a moment when you thought this approach is not working, we will throw this out and do something different . . . go out and play football, go for a walk. You cannot do that now. You could be very individualistic, you could be quite radical. The child who is out of the classroom for whatever reason, he has missed a piece of academic work. It's not the case that he needed to be out of the classroom for space. I think there are good things about the National Curriculum. This type of school should be aiming to provide the child with a timetable and expect them to be on task. What I think is sad is that there aren't other types of school available for some children.

It was not always a case of whether or not the curriculum was appropriate, but more the whole classroom situation created by the National Curriculum: 'The pressure of the National Curriculum makes these children stand out like sore thumbs.'

Specific mention of local management of schools was less common than more general concerns about the relative lack of educational psychologist time and support services since the advent of LMS. However, one head teacher summarized the dilemma of balancing the needs of the individual with that of the group, in a context where the financial consequences of doing so or not were very evident:

> I think we have sharpened up our awareness of the effect of a disruptive child in a classroom . . . local management of schools has done that. I think that's right, I think that I should be aware of that and protect the other 28 or 30 children in the class. But, I wouldn't want to be in a situation where I was saying that I didn't want to work with a child because of the financial implications . . . There is a fine dividing line between the two things I am saying.

The last quote was from a head teacher of an affluent suburban junior school. He felt that all the LEA and government were interested in was making it harder for schools to exclude pupils. He stressed that schools needed more support with some pupils.

Summary and conclusions

The accounts given by teachers of the behaviours of the excluded children often show a picture of children presenting very extreme behaviour, relative to their experience of teaching in mainstream schools. Nearly all the teachers made clear distinctions between 'naughty' behaviour, special educational needs and what they viewed as 'disturbed' behaviour. A great deal of sympathy was usually shown towards these children, but there was a tendency to believe that the children's needs could only be met by either more staff and, in some cases, more specialist staff. Many of the accounts from teachers included references to the practical difficulties of catering for the needs of other children in the same class, many of whom had a range of special educational needs, health needs and social circumstances to consider. The behaviour of the excluded children was reported to stand out against other members of the group in most cases. In many cases excluded children even stood out as individuals in a teacher's career. These accounts could of course be interpreted as justifications after the event, although there was a remarkable similarity between the accounts from home and school of the child's behaviour. The issue in dispute was usually about whether an exclusion from school was an appropriate response to the child's behaviour.

One might have expected greater distinctions between the children who had less serious exclusions investigated (fixed term) and those who had the more serious ones (indefinite and permanent). However, many of the children investigated on the basis of a fixed term exclusion subsequently had more serious exclusions or were found to have had more serious exclusions from previous schools. Thus although there were a small number of children who might be viewed as primarily 'naughty', rather than 'needy', the distinction between the characteristics of these two groups was by no means as clear as one might have hoped. Head teachers and class teachers did not disagree to any great extent about the difficulties a child was presenting in the classroom and, indeed, in the whole school environment. Yet some class teachers clearly did not want the child in question excluded. Head teachers usually showed a great deal of sympathy for the child they excluded, and had often spent a great deal of time with them when they could not be contained in the classroom. However, it was clear that they felt that this could not go on indefinitely, in that they had a range of duties to perform which were not compatible with caring for an individual child.

Excluding a child from school, or being the class teacher of such a child, was obviously an upsetting experience for the teachers interviewed. It was often acknowledged that almost all such primary age children could be catered for with more space and more teachers. The National Curriculum was felt to be a restriction in catering flexibly for the needs of some children, both in mainstream schools and in special schools. Head teachers were obviously aware of the costs of catering for difficult children and LMS had made the financial costs very clear, but there was no evidence that financial costs were a key issue in deciding whether or not to exclude a child. Some head teachers mentioned that parents had taken children away from the school before the individual was finally excluded. Resource issues were thus usually in the background in a number of ways: resources were lost to some schools when other parents took their children away, and ultimately it was the lack of appropriate resources, both in terms of staff time and expertise, as well as space, which explains why exclusion was taken as an option. Thus in sum, the changes in education set in motion by the Education Reform Act 1988 and continued since, are responsible for creating both resource pressures and curriculum pressures which in turn create practical difficulties in managing the behaviour of some children. In certain circumstances, these difficulties could result in the exclusion of a child, a decision which was much less likely in primary schools before the Education Reform Act 1988.

Seven

Summary and conclusions to Section 2

The evidence of a rise in official records of primary school children excluded from school is clear. Most local authorities now have a small but growing group of young children for whom it is difficult to cater appropriately. We have seen that primary school children are excluded from school for behaviour which is deemed 'unacceptable' in that school. This may seem and indeed is a relative concept. Undoubtedly some children may have had a fixed term exclusion which would not have been the response to their behaviour in another school, a conclusion also reached by Franklyn-Stokes (1989). However, the children who are eventually permanently excluded do display behaviours which are out of the ordinary. As we have seen, such behaviours are very often physically and verbally aggressive and thus directly impinge on other individuals' sense of security and wellbeing in a school. Such children are unusually not at all compliant with adults and have very poor skills of social interaction with their peers. Some behaviours can be extremely difficult to contain in a mainstream classroom and school, with many of the children investigated absconding from the school site. However, when children behave in this way they are not simply 'naughty', they are telling adults something about how they feel. In a sense they may be asking adults to set some controls and limits for them and thus help them feel safe (Carroll 1995). Schools are part of the socialization process and this does include promoting sociable behaviour in children, which will include them with their peers, rather than exclude them from contact with their peer group altogether. With unusually vulnerable children there are simply not enough adults (or space sometimes) in mainstream primary schools to provide the individual attention often needed.

Common variables

Figure 7.1 attempts to bring together the key variables which were common in many of the case studies of children. The most common variables were family breakdown, special educational need (EBD) and social services involvement in the family. Nearly half the children had spent time 'looked after' by the local authority during the year in which they were excluded. This experience tended to add to the disruptions in their schooling, which was sometimes compounded when information was not passed on to schools which could be critical in preparing staff to cater for the child appropriately. Figure 7.1 shows a degree of predictability about the kind of individual and home circumstances in which an exclusion from school is possible, especially the most severe category. It also illustrates variables in the school circumstances which are likely to play a part in the whole situation. The circumstances surrounding the decision to exclude a primary school child (particularly permanently) are complex. Figure 7.1 attempts to depict this complexity. The areas of overlap in the diagram are there to represent the fact that these variables are part of a dynamic situation, in which there is interaction. Thus the stresses in a child's home and school life will go a long way towards explaining their behaviour. How this behaviour is then managed (or not) in a school relates to the circumstances in that school and importantly the wellbeing, attitudes and capabilities of the head teacher. The inclusion of race as one of the factors in these sets of variables is emotive, but as we have seen, Black children (specifically African-Caribbean boys) are overrepresented in available exclusion statistics. However, it must also be considered how many of the other variables are present in cases where Black children are excluded from school, variables which are common when White children are excluded.

It is proposed that it is the interaction between the sets of variables depicted in Figure 7.1 which largely explains primary school exclusion, although the influence of social policy is important both in influencing the circumstances of children and their families, as well as schools, and thus in framing how events are construed by those with the power to exclude. Such a set of variables may be interpreted in more than one way, for example they could be used to compile a profile of the least desirable child for a school (operating in a quasi-market) to admit. On the other hand, such variables could be used to inform the planning process for children who have to change schools or be reintegrated to school after some disruption in their lives.

Stress

A particularly useful concept which relates the behaviour of a child as an individual to his/her environment in the broadest sense, is that of stress. Stress in schools and homes will remain a lasting impression from the field research. It is perhaps fair to say that in everyday terms, adults overlook

Figure 7.1 Common variables in the characteristics and circumstances of primary age children excluded from school

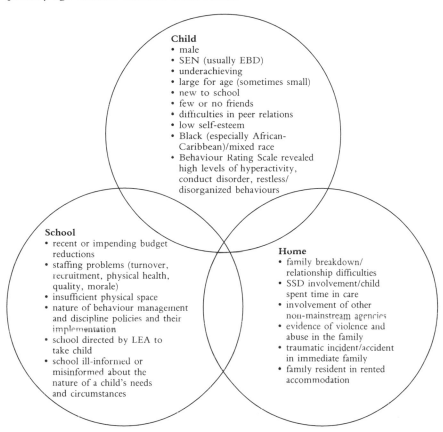

the stresses to which children, especially young children, are exposed. Although there are debates about the definition of the term 'stress' (Rutter 1981), as well as its possible impact on children (Chandler 1981), there is little doubt that children exposed to multiple stresses are more likely to display 'unacceptable behaviour' (Rutter 1978). In this context it is important to emphasize that most of the children reported upon in Section 2 of this book were subjected to multiple stresses, with an average of 6.7 per child out of a possible total of 12 (see. Table 4.2). Children in the same family in the research did not necessarily have the same response to these stresses, and some appeared not to have any response at all to the same circumstances. For example, while Andy's response to stress was 'acting out' and attention-seeking behaviours, his older brother (aged 12) had taken on the parenting role and generally acted in a way which could be described as responsible beyond his years.

Quamma and Greenburg (1994) report that the relationship between stressful life events and psychological maladjustment is well established, but that the majority of the research has focused upon adults and adolescents. Children who have adverse responses to stress may behave in ways which are often polarized into neurotic behaviour and 'acting out' or other forms of externalizing behaviour (Goldstein 1994). It is the acting-out behaviour which is often seen as most problematic in schools (Quamma and Greenburg 1994). However, Chandler *et al.* (1985) use a more complex model to show four common patterns of response to stress in childhood: the repressed child and the passive-aggressive child, the dependent child and the impulsive child. It is the impulsive child with his/her overactive and acting-out behaviour which best describes the behaviours reported in this research.

In attempting to identify why some children are more susceptible to stressors than others, parenting skills are often emphasized:

> despite the harshness of life that the families encounter, some parents appear to be able to foster or enhance in their children the confidence, self control, determination, flexibility and cognitive skills that accompany the development of competence and positive adaptation. These appear to be important precursors to the establishment of stress-resistance in children.
>
> (Garmezy 1981, cited in Chandler 1985: 114)

The concept of competence is central to Garmezy's work, and he has developed a series of indicators which relate to the competence of individual children. In relation to the children in this study these are very pertinent indicators:

(1) *Effectiveness in work, play and love*; satisfactory educational and occupational progress; peer regard and friendship;
(2) *Healthy expectations* and the belief that 'good outcomes' will follow from the imposition of effort and initiative; an orientation to success rather than the anticipation of failure in performing tasks; a realistic level of aspiration unbeclouded by unrealistically high or low goal setting behaviour;
(3) *Self-esteem*, feelings of personal worthiness, a proper evaluative set towards self and sense of 'fate control', that is, the belief that one can control events in one's environment rather than be a passive victim of them (an internal as opposed to an external locus of control);
(4) *Self-discipline*, as revealed by the ability to delay gratification and to maintain future-orientedness;
(5) *Control and regulation of impulsive drives*; the ability to adopt a reflective as opposed to an impulsive style in coping with problem situations;
(6) *The ability to think abstractly*; to approach new situations and to be able to attempt alternate solutions to a problem.

                                         (quoted in Chandler 1985: 115)

From the data collected in this research it is possible to comment with greatest confidence upon the first three indicators as described above. The great majority of the children excluded from school were viewed as having special educational needs, their home circumstances were frequently disrupted and unsupportive, and their peer group interactions were often negative. In these circumstances they were unable to achieve the effectiveness in work, play and love referred to above. They were frequently described as having low self-esteem and as avoiding possible failure by not trying with their school work in the first place. Descriptions of their behaviour would indicate difficulties in self-control and discipline, as well as problem-solving skills. The restrictions and pressures placed on young children (Blenkin and Kelly 1994) by the National Curriculum may have helped emphasize the difficulties of some of them, to themselves, their teachers and their peers.

Explaining primary school exclusion

The evidence suggests that changes in education policy and, specifically, the introduction of a quasi-market into the education system are only part of the explanation for the rise in records of primary school exclusion. These changes have certainly produced a climate in schools which may not only be less sympathetic to the more challenging children but also have less capacity to cater for them more flexibly. In particular, the way individual children are funded under LMS and the relatively small amount of resources available to support children with special educational needs who do not have a statement, as well as the requirements of the National Curriculum, create practical pressures and restrictions for schools trying to cater for them. Added to these issues is the pressure from parents and public opinion more generally, in relation to both standards of behaviour and academic standards, which makes it difficult for schools to show the kind of tolerance which is needed to work with the most challenging children. However, changes in other social policies (integration of children with SEN and reduction in residential care) have exacerbated this situation by placing more challenging children in mainstream schools at a time when there are reduced incentives, as well as capacity, to cope with them.

There are also a number of socio-economic changes which help to explain why some children and families may be suffering from more stress than in previous decades, in particular increasing family breakdown and relative poverty, as well as long-term unemployment. These socio-economic and policy changes have helped to make schools more pressurized and stressful environments for teachers, and for some children too. These pressures are slightly different in primary schools, in comparison with secondary schools, particularly in relation to the aspect of external examinations and the prominence given by the media to league tables of results. If the publication of Key Stage 1 and 2 test results (at the ages of 7 and 11) is given more prominence in future, as seems likely, it may further increase the level of disincentives for teachers to concentrate most effort upon the children who are likely to bring least credit to a school. Most primary school teachers in the research were only too well aware of the pressures and expectations placed upon them, but there was still evidence in the research of a strong belief that, given appropriate resources, they would be willing to work with almost all (even all) children.

Available evidence suggests that the exclusion of a child from primary school was rare before the 1990s (Galloway *et al.* 1982) because such children were likely to have been sent to a special school, or perhaps received more support in various residential environments (York *et al.* 1972). Current social policies would discourage these options. However, there has not yet been enough thought given to the reality of coping with some of the more severe 'acting out' behaviours displayed by the most distressed children in primary schools. Such children may not have any other safe opportunity to display these behaviours, apart from in school. The training of teachers in behaviour management is still very limited and some primary schools lack the physical space, both inside and outside the classroom, to provide some of the kinds of individual and small-group work needed. All of these factors have led to a situation in which the threshold of tolerance in primary school teachers for aberrant behaviours may have changed, so that a fixed term exclusion becomes a more expedient and acceptable response to 'unacceptable' behaviour than it once was. The increase in the number of permanently excluded primary school children in and of itself may also help to make this option one that is now known about and considered in primary schools, when once it was probably not. Section 3 of the book will consider some of the institutional responses aimed at the management of children's behaviour. Some of these responses are directly related to the issue of school exclusion; others tackle broader issues about promoting appropriate behaviour in children both inside school and outside, at home and in the community.

Section 3

The responses

Responses: an introduction

A comment by the mother of 7-year-old twin boys, Lewis and Jerry, makes an obvious but important point: 'there should be something between being in or out . . . there should be something on the Tuesday if they are thrown out on a Monday.' Like the majority of the children in the case studies, Lewis and Jerry eventually went back to school. They both had fixed term exclusions, followed by an indefinite exclusion; they had also been excluded from lunchtimes for a whole school year. When they returned to school after their indefinite exclusions they were put in a part of the school library with a home tutor for 25 hours a week. They received draft statements for EBD at the end of this same school year. These children missed the equivalent of a term of schooling during their last year of infant school, all possibilities of mixing with their peers at lunchtimes for the whole year and were effectively on an internal (in-school) exclusion when they returned to school. Furthermore their future schooling was still very uncertain at the end of the school year, with neither child being in receipt of a junior school place, less than two months before they were due to start this phase of their education. The response of the education department to these children was slow, as Parsons *et al.* (1994) have also found: apart from home tuition there was very little on offer for these children and their family. Like many of the excluded children, Lewis and Jerry had special educational needs: they had suffered the breakdown of their parents' relationship and had not adjusted well to their mother's remarriage. The education service has a clear remit to respond to the special educational needs of these children, but the broader issues about family dynamics are more clearly the remit of social services and health-based agencies, such as child and family guidance.

Halsey (1993) has highlighted the potential of primary schools as a site from which to operate support systems for parents and carers which could improve the quality of childhood, which Young and Halsey (1995) believe is necessary. In writing of school-based programmes aimed at preventing the development of entrenched emotional and behavioural problems in children, Durlak (1995: ix) says: 'Schools are a natural environment for prevention programmes because most children attend schools, and through them an infrastructure exists for reaching large numbers of children in their formative years.'

However Chapter 8 argues that using schools as a base for wider community programmes would require the reallocation and reorganization of existing family support workers and resources. Primary schools, as Webb (1994) has so aptly described, are labouring under a 'deluge of directives' and are widely recognized to be underresourced relative to secondary education. A family support worker is a different sort of person with a different role and professional training from a teacher, and rightly so. By expecting teachers to take on such roles it may be not only an unrealistic additional burden, but also potentially in conflict with other professionals trained and experienced in this sort of work.

Prevention and prevalence

The concept of prevention in relation to the development of behaviour problems in children and young people may be variously defined (see for example, Utting 1995; Durlak 1995). Primary prevention usually involves interventions with normal populations, such as in a mainstream school, with the aim of precluding the occurrence of problems. Other types of prevention include intervention during the early development of difficulties, before they achieve the status of a major problem or 'disorder', or work with individuals who have already got to this stage (Durlak 1995). The need for primary prevention is obvious when one considers the very large proportions of children likely to experience behaviour problems as shown by prevalence studies, or indeed estimates of the proportion of children likely to have a special educational need.

Table R.1 summarizes some of these estimates and compares them with the number and proportion of primary age children excluded from school. Such figures may require us to reflect upon how successful schools actually are in catering for the overwhelming majority of children, although whether they are really 'included' requires some debate. Inclusive education is sometimes seen as a radical concept in that it is based on a critical view of how our education system is currently operating, and thus highlights the need for change. Inclusive education would not start from the premise that all children should be taught in large groups, but with special provision to integrate children who cannot cope with this. Evidence can be offered that the current system does not work for a large proportion of children, who

Table R.1 Proportion of permanent primary school exclusions compared with selected prevalence studies and children with SEN

Permanent primary school exclusions 1993–4[1]	
1 in 3,270 primary age children	or 0.031% of primary age children
Selected prevalence studies[2]	
ADD, with/without hyperactivity	2.2 → 9.9%
Conduct 'disorder'	4.0 → 10.0%
Development 'disorders'	10.0 → 20.0%
Behavioural 'deviance'	10.6 → 25.4%
Special educational need (SEN)[3]	
Likely to need a statement of SEN	2.0% (2.49% in January 1994)
Likely to need SEN support (incl. statemented children) at some time in their schooling	20.0%
Likely to need SEN support at any one time	16.6%

1 Source: Parsons *et al.* 1995
2 Source: Rutter *et al.* 1975; CPPRG 1992; Goldstein 1994
3 Source: DES/WO 1989

make this known through their underachievement and disaffected behaviour. Inclusive education would start by recognizing the diversity of all pupils' learning needs (Wedell 1995). The principle of inclusive education is increasingly accepted in many areas of the world, where numerous examples of good practice can be found (Mittler 1995).

However, whether we are working with goals of integration or inclusion the central dilemma in relation to children at risk of exclusion is how to understand and respond to their behaviour. Peagram (1995) has noted the lack of agreement about the definition of EBD among special educators, as well as the mistaken notion that EBD can be equated with other forms of special educational need. This is an important issue in relation to developing appropriate responses. The child who may be viewed as disruptive or naughty, or experiencing some emotional stress within normal bounds may respond well to consistent and appropriate behaviour management in school. Children who display behaviour which may arise from more severe or prolonged stress may have more difficulty in responding likewise (Hanko 1994). It can be difficult for teachers to make this distinction in practice. A further consideration is that of the continuity and change in the behaviour of children (Badger 1985). Although it is generally accepted that early intervention is likely to be most successful in the prevention of major behaviour problems, there are some questions about how accurately we can diagnose the need for intervention. Thus, although there is continuity and consistency in behaviour over a number of years with some children, with others there is evidence of variability and change (Upton 1981). In other words, some behaviour problems are a phase of development for the

majority of children. Yet this may only serve to underline that primary prevention is of paramount importance in the primary school, as is accurate diagnosis in secondary prevention. Many of the positive approaches to behaviour management within the education service can play a part in this.

The need is clear for integrated programmes which address the promotion of appropriate behaviour in young children, and which reach out beyond the confines of the requirements of the classroom and the school (CPPRG 1992; Maginnis 1993). Yet some workers in the helping professions think of behaviour modification as limited to a one-to-one 'clinical' type of activity (Herbert 1985), rather than the ecosystemic approaches which are more popular within a school setting. Lloyd Bennett (1995) points to the relative infancy of parent behaviour management programmes, in comparison with the attention focused upon behaviour management in schools. He says that school-based behaviour management programmes may well produce well ordered, task focused classrooms, but that children will not necessarily behave appropriately in other situations without the structure provided by these programmes. That is, school-based programmes may be able to provide the external controls which will guide children into patterns of positive and appropriate behaviour in the classroom. However, such programmes will not be able to provide sufficiently for some of the children from home environments where they have not been able to internalize positive, appropriate and socially acceptable behaviour.

Programmes like FAST Track (Families and Schools Together), developed in the United States, take a multisystemic approach in attempting to promote the development of appropriate behaviour in all of the key areas of a young child's life (CPPRG 1992: 513): 'A preventive model requires not only the development of appropriate social-cognitive and behavioral skills in the child and parent, but also the development of a healthy bond between the family and school, child and family, and child and school.' The FAST Track model includes parent training, home visiting/case management, social skills training, academic tutoring and teacher-based classroom intervention. It takes a long-range approach to intervention and prevention. Such integrated approaches are not common in Britain, although a wide variety of either school or home-based initiatives to address the behaviour of children and young people can be found. The following two chapters will consider some of the approaches in the education service, as well as other services, to behaviour problems and the exclusion from school of primary age children.

Eight

What can education service-based initiatives do?

Background

The Elton Report (DES/WO 1989) notes the long-term and international nature of adult concerns about the school-based behaviour of children and young people, although there is a lack of comparative data for previous periods. This perception of indiscipline among children in school (and indeed in society more generally) is arguably fuelled by the media and the intermittent moral panics (after Cohen 1980) which can erupt after particular events. This is not to minimize the effect on teachers feeling that they are being prevented from doing their job properly, or the effects of sustaining an attack from a pupil. The Elton report (DES/WO 1989: 5) advises that we have realistic aims about behaviour management:

> Reducing bad behaviour is a realistic aim. Eliminating it completely is not. Historical and international comparisons help to illustrate this obvious but important point. Children have a need to discover where the boundaries of acceptable behaviour lie. It is natural for them to test these boundaries to confirm their location and, in some cases, for the excitement of challenge. The proper answer to such testing is to confirm the existence of the boundaries, and to do so firmly, unequivocally and at once.

Exclusion from school, particularly a permanent exclusion, is the ultimate sanction for a school to use in relation to unacceptable or inappropriate behaviour; it was an option rarely utilised, or at least recorded as such, for primary school pupils until the 1990s. As noted in Chapter 2, Galloway *et al.* (1982) made the immediate association between special education needs and the kind of behaviour which might occasion a primary school exclusion. This is an association which, as we have seen from the research evidence presented in Section 2, has proved to be valid in many cases. Thus the response of the education service must be both to address the issues of order and discipline, while recognizing that special educational need may be a factor for some children. Behaviour management and support structures for schools, individual teachers and individual children become a critical focus in relation to preventing exclusions.

National and LEA initiatives

The 'Pupils with problems' documents (DfE 1994a), which followed the implementation of the Education Act 1993, attempt to build on the findings of the Elton Report. These six circulars outline proper procedure and provision for children in a range of difficulties or disadvantaged circumstances. One possibility is to cater for excluded children outside ordinary schools in off-site units, now known as pupil referral units (PRUs). Some LEAs have been quick to establish PRUs as a main part of their response to excluded pupils, while others have chosen other programmes such as those run by Cities in Schools, a national charity. The prime intention of PRUs is to return pupils to mainstream schools or to work (OFSTED 1995). Yet the first inspections of PRUs indicated that a return to school was too low a priority in the way they were actually working (p. 7). There are over 300 PRUs nationally catering for excluded pupils and other children out of school, mostly in the secondary school age range. PRUs are not always seen as an alternative for primary age children, many of whom have to make do with a few hours of home tuition a week. Thus, a return to the original school, a new mainstream school placement, or a special school/ unit placement are the real alternatives for primary age children. Initiatives which address behaviour in mainstream schools are of great importance for primary age children at risk of exclusion.

GEST (Grants for Education Service and Training) have produced a number of national programmes on the theme of truancy and disaffection, which in some ways relate to the issue of exclusion. The underlying issue in all of these projects is pupil behaviour, disaffected pupils tending to behave in a way which is perceived as difficult to manage at best, or 'unacceptable' at worst. By adjusting or changing what is on offer in school, or how a situation is managed, it is often hoped that some affection for school might be created and thus more acceptable behaviour (see Barrett (1989) for a discussion of the origins and nature of disaffection in the primary school).

Although many GEST projects focus on secondary age pupils, some LEAs are reported as viewing the transition period from primary to secondary school as a crucial time of adjustment for some pupils (Learmonth 1995). Learmonth's evaluation of the Truancy and Disaffected Pupils GEST programme provides a useful overview of the range of projects conducted across the country, as well as examples of good practice. However, Learmonth's study is critical of the year-on-year funding, which he says is 'not helpful to good planning, . . . not efficient, and . . . [does] not encourage long-term evaluation of projects' (p. 4).

An 'inclusion' project

As an illustration of a GEST-funded project we will now briefly refer to the findings from a GEST funded 'inclusion' project which presents some of the key planning and service principles for LEAs trying to work to include pupils and thus reduce exclusion. The project operated during the 1994–5 academic year and had the following aim: 'to reduce exclusions by identifying "at risk of permanent exclusion" students and to work with students, parents and school staff to identify and develop creative strategies which enable "at risk" students to continue attendance at school' (Fox 1995: 2). The project involved senior teachers from seven schools (five secondary, two primary) who each identified one 'at risk' student from each school. Parent, child and teacher views of the situation were analysed and compiled by the project team, with a view to identifying appropriate responses and strategies to identified needs. The project identified a 'Menu of possibilities' for schools to use, as follows:

Step 1 (little or no resource implication)

schools can:

- use an information gathering pack in order to plan effectively
- provide an 'exit' card/bolthole for particular at risk pupils
- arrange tracking by a trusted and supportive colleague
- provide staff support group
- make use of outreach from PRU
- make alternative arrangements for less structured times in the day
- arrange peer support
- set up home/school link/record
- involve EP and/or FWO in any of the above

Step 2 (greater resource implication)

schools can:

- provide different educational provision for some/all of the time
- provide a calm, consistent teacher
- facilitate access to counselling
- provide access to a social skills training group
- make flexible arrangements
- encourage parent involvement
- provide life skills/vocational curriculum (disapplication of National Curriculum for some?)

(Fox 1995: 4–5)

Not all schools will need reminding about all of these possibilities. However, such GEST projects can help develop and build upon existing good practice and enable other schools to take on such a 'Menu of possibilities' for their more difficult pupils.

LEA: behaviour support

Educational psychologists (EPs) have the potential to offer support to schools on behaviour management, but it is a potential that is not always realized in practice. Primary schools may often get only two half days of EP time a term to deal with their concerns. Schools in our study varied in their appreciation of the service as it now stands, but the common complaint was that the amount of time available made preventive and developmental work extremely difficult within the ordinary EP time allocation for a school. Such time tended to be used for reviews of children with statements, and requests for observation and advice with a view to formal assessment for special educational needs. There were limited opportunities for INSET (in-service training) in relation to behaviour management. Teachers often spoke of prioritizing the list of children who they wanted to consult the educational psychologist about. Some teachers also reported that their educational psychologist was more useful in relation to learning difficulties rather than behavioural difficulties (although this is a false distinction). GEST-funded projects and LEA-run behaviour support services offered an important opportunity for additional support for behaviour management in schools, and in such cases offered the potential of a preventive role for educational psychologists.

Some LEAs have established behaviour support services, which tend to vary in organization and style, according to their origins, funding and staffing. One of a number of possible behaviour support structures will now be described. In one LEA visited in the research, all of the behaviour support was focused on primary schools. One of the three established teams was based with the educational psychology service and took referrals from this service. The team consisted of two teachers of advisory status, two classroom assistants, a half-time EP and some secretarial support. The original plan was to include a half-time family worker, with funding from the social services department. Towards the end of the second year of operation of this service it had still not been possible to appoint this worker because of lack of funding. One of the advisory teachers said of this: 'as a team we feel strongly that we need the family worker . . . without him/her, it minimizes the impact of our work'. As there was no family worker it was up to the head teacher to inform and attempt to involve the family in the proposed programme. This is a process which some head teachers were not able to do very well. In the worst scenario the following might happen:

> [There is] a formal meeting [in the school] with everybody sitting round and in comes usually a young single mum to meet all these

people. To hear them berate the child and say how awful the child is and that's why all the people are here to help him . . . There's always this undertone of blame. Sometimes there's no way round it without a family worker. I often marvel at how cooperative families are in these circumstances.

The spokesperson for this project and, indeed, for others visited, emphasized the importance of having a family worker with a different and distinct remit from that of the school and who would provide the important link between home and school.

What might a behaviour support team do?

Behaviour support teams may work with individual children, groups or classes as well as whole schools. Some time-limited projects investigated were attached to clusters of schools (i.e. a secondary school and the primary feeder schools). Whatever the remit, such a team will provide the additional human resource needed in a busy classroom, but more importantly they will pass on ideas and skills to improve behaviour management. Although the entry point to a school is often an individual creating a great deal of concern, a skilled behaviour support teacher will be able to identify other individuals who need help and support as well as whole-school issues. As one behaviour support teacher said, 'for every single one of our acting out cases we have spotted an elective mute . . . Very soon we stop talking about that case and move on to that class and then to the whole school.'

Support teachers may have a wide-ranging brief, which can include work with the child referred, the teacher, other children in the class and indeed the whole school. Some teams may also have support assistants to complement the work of the behaviour support teachers. In one team investigated, the support assistants went into schools for different sessions from the behaviour support teachers and worked with both the individual child in the classroom and the classroom assistant, where appropriate. In this way, like the support teacher, the support assistant contributed to in-service training for classroom assistants. The role of a family worker on such a team is primarily to support and work with the parents/carers of children with behaviour problems in school. Their role may also include establishing positive parent support for all parents in a particular school. The team EP has an overall planning, coordinating and monitoring role, as well as individual input where the skills and expertise of a psychologist are required (see for example, Bryan and Simpson 1995).

Whole-school policies for behaviour management

It is at the level of the school that positive approaches have to make an impact and are likely to cover related issues of discipline, bullying, equal opportunities and special educational needs provision, as well as behaviour more generally within schools. At the level of the group, the focus is largely about strategies of classroom management of these issues, within the policy context agreed by the school. Some individuals will not be effectively managed within whole-school or classroom strategies and will need individual education plans (IEPs), as required by the Code of Practice for special educational needs (DfE 1994b). In addition, staff need advice and guidance on how to reduce conflict, prevent face-to-face violence, and deal with such events when they occur.

Whole-school behaviour policies have been promoted in the 1990s so that the boundaries of acceptable behaviour are not left to the individual teacher to decide. According to DfE circular 8/94 (DfE 1994b), such policies should be developed by the head teacher, class teachers and non-teaching staff in consultation with the school governors, with the governing body taking a clear lead in proposing principles and standards. Parents and pupils should be involved in discussion of the development of a policy, which should also be featured in the annual report to parents and in the school prospectus. The precise content of a school's behaviour policy is left up to the individual school to decide.

Although schools have always had rules and accompanying reward and punishment systems, not all schools have had behaviour policies. The Elton Report (DES/WO 1989) suggested that schools which simply have a long list of prohibitions and no consistent behaviour policy were more likely to be troubled by bad behaviour than those which had harmonized all the features of the institution with regard to behaviour. The Elton Report found that schools which relied on punishments as a deterrent to unwanted behaviour were likely to be disappointed. Both Rutter *et al.* (1979) and Mortimore *et al.* (1988) confirm these kind of findings.

Learmonth (1995: 76) has reported many benefits from whole-school approaches to behaviour management, including a decrease in the number of exclusions from a school. In contrast Peagram (1995: 9) refers to increasing evidence that the widespread adoption of whole-school behaviour policies and structured approaches to discipline may actually relate to the recorded increase in exclusions, as well as increased referrals for statementing of children for EBD. Clearly the sensitivity and understanding with which such policies are implemented has a great deal to do with their effects. In order to reduce exclusions, policies need to be both consistent but flexible in the kinds of exceptional circumstances which could precipitate an exclusion.

Examples of contrasting behaviour management strategies

Changing the way an institution operates is a difficult task, and for some schools this is aided by adopting a particular behaviour management strategy, such as 'Assertive Discipline' or the 'Circle Time' approach, both of which come with training packages which can fit into a school's INSET programme. There are a variety of other ideas and packages but these two approaches were most commonly referred to during our field research. They also provide a useful philosophical contrast in terms of thinking about behaviour management in the school setting. Assertive Discipline, as the name of the strategy implies, is very much about adults (i.e. teachers) taking a strong, consistent lead in their approach to setting the boundaries for acceptable and appropriate behaviour for children in school. Circle Time, in contrast, starts from a different philosophical viewpoint, in creating periods of time in which adults and children have more equal status, within a framework in which opportunities are made and encouragement given for all children to communicate, experience success and be rewarded.

Assertive Discipline (Canter and Canter 1992)

Assertive Discipline is an idea which was originally developed in the United States, with the first book on the matter published in 1976 (*Assertive Discipline: a Take-Charge Approach for Today's Educator*). An updated version of one of the key documents which outlines this approach (Canter and Canter 1992: 14) defines the assertive teacher as 'one who clearly and firmly communicates her expectations to her students, and is prepared to reinforce her words with appropriate actions. She responds to students in a manner that maximises her potential to get her own needs to teach met, but in no way violates the best interests of the students.'

The overall aim of the book is to provide a basis upon which to establish a well-ordered classroom, which teachers can then adapt to their own personal style and the particular needs of their students. It is suggested that other theories and approaches to managing school behaviour can be integrated into the Assertive Discipline approach. The book opens with the reminder that the teacher has the right to teach and that pupils (referred to as students) have the right to learn in a classroom free from disruptive behaviour, and it pinpoints the pupil's rights in the classroom.

Assertive Discipline is based on the belief that 'most children can behave when they want to do so' (p. 19). The system acknowledges that some children with special educational needs and impoverished backgrounds (emotionally as well as materially) will find it more difficult to behave appropriately, but points out that a major block to the success of such children is whether the teacher believes they can help them. Agreeing and setting clear, consistent behavioural expectations in a school is the basis of the Assertive Discipline approach.

Key aspects of the strategy

A classroom discipline plan is a key part of the whole approach, consisting of rules which children must follow at all times, positive recognition for pupils following the rules and consequences when pupils choose not to follow the rules. The word 'choose' is crucial here because in the strategy the child is made aware, through a reminder about the rules and the consequences of not following them, that they are choosing the consequences if they continue the behaviour. Sample classroom discipline plans are offered, which can be amended and reworded according to the circumstances and age range of particular schools. Individual rewards and whole-class rewards are suggested. Individuals may be offered stickers and merits, positive letters home and so on. Whole classes can work towards a whole-class reward, such as a particular activity or trip out of school, for good behaviour. In the latter strategy peer pressure is made use of in order to attain the desired goal. Progress towards such a whole-class reward might be recorded by marbles in a jar for every house point or other recognition a member of the class obtains. Assertive Discipline makes the distinction between rewarding good behaviour and 'bribery'. A bribe is given to entice somebody to do something they would not normally do, perhaps because it is not enjoyable or not in the individual's best interest; furthermore, a bribe is given in anticipation of a behaviour. A reward, on the other hand, is given as a result of a wanted behaviour and in recognition that it is in the individual's best interest.

Individualized behaviour plans

Canter and Canter (1992: 227) recognize that the framework they provide will not work for some pupils. Such individuals are likely to need an individualized behaviour plan, which specifies:

- the specific behaviours expected of the pupil;
- meaningful consequences to be imposed if the pupil does not choose to engage in the appropriate behaviour;
- meaningful positive recognition to be given when the pupil does behave appropriately.

Canter and Canter acknowledge that the natural inclination of teachers dealing with difficult students may be to 'come down hard' on them, but they view this as a short-sighted approach. At the most basic level, such children are likely to try and get the teacher's attention one way or another, so that paying the child attention for appropriate, rather than inappropriate behaviour is a more positive way forward. For the pupil where nothing seems to work, they advise a close look at what is happening to see whether there is a pattern. They suggest that perhaps positive behaviour is being ignored or the teacher may not be following through consistently with the original plan. As Canter and Canter say, 'in reality, nothing will work when a teacher does not consistently provide consequences to the student' (p. 19). They believe that the myth of 'the good teacher' ought to be debunked, as not only does it place a burden of guilt on teachers, but it prevents teachers asking for additional help for pupils who need it. The Assertive Discipline system also emphasizes the importance of obtaining support from parents for the school's behavioural expectations, particularly with children who have an individualized behaviour plan. The system advises getting in touch with parents at the first signs of a problem, getting support from senior staff and recording the problematic behaviours and steps taken to deal with them. In-school 'suspension' (that is, internal exclusion on the school site) is suggested for children whose behaviour is very disruptive in the classroom. It is suggested that this type of suspension is likely to be particularly effective with children who prefer an unsupervised out-of-school suspension. It is advised that such suspensions should occur in appropriate facilities, that is properly ventilated rooms with supervision, rather than in bookstores and closets.

Circle Time (Mosley 1993)

Circle Time has developed out of longer traditions: people have been sitting in circles discussing issues since ancient times. At the most basic level, circles are a practical way for all members of a group to make eye contact with each other. They can also help to make individuals feel they are on a more equal footing within a discussion. One version of this approach can be found in Mosley's book, *Turn Your School Round*. As Mosley (1993) points out, 'Quality Circles' have been used in industry since the 1960s, in order to try and develop a better relationship between management and shopfloor staff. The contrast between the philosophy of the Circle Time approach and that of Assertive Discipline is apparent if one compares the following quote from Mosley with the opening quote in the last section (Canter and Canter 1992: 14):

> Circle Time is a democratic and creative approach used to consider a wide range of issues affecting the whole school community; teaching staff, children, support staff, parents and governors . . . In the school setting, the Circle Time method involves all participants sitting in a circle and taking equal responsibility for the solving of problems and the issues that they have highlighted themselves . . . The teacher adopts a facilitative role in order to encourage participants to feel that they too have the authority and control to solve the behaviour, learning or relationship problems that concern them . . .
>
> (Mosley 1993: 9)

Key aspects of the strategy

Circle Time aims to build upon a wide range of basic skills for children and address whole-school issues. A central aim of Circle Time is self-esteem building. Circle Time sets out to develop and enhance children's self-esteem through the use of a range of activities and structures which set out to motivate individuals to share thoughts and feelings in a safe environment and to create a collective responsibility for promoting self-esteem and positive behaviour. The emphasis in the opening sections of Mosley's book are initially upon self-esteem and positive behaviour, but she also links Circle Time to the very specific requirements of parts of the National Curriculum. During Circle Time 'Golden Rules' are discussed, established and revised. These rules are developed in full cooperation between all staff (teaching and support) and children. These rules are then displayed in each classroom, staffroom, dining hall and playground. The rules may not all focus on exactly the same issues, but nevertheless will fall broadly under the philosophical 'umbrella' of: respect for myself, respect for others, respect for property. Circle Time is then used to devise an incentives policy to promote and reinforce the Golden Rules.

Children 'beyond'

Like Canter, Mosley recognizes that a particular whole-school system or approach to behaviour management will not work for all children. She describes such children as 'beyond' normal incentives and sanctions and lunch-time policies. However, she cautions against too much haste in naming such children. She says that such children will be obvious once the Circle Time system has been fully established for some time. Mosley (p. 38) describes these children as:

> confused children, whose basic emotional and physical needs have not been or are not being met. Within many of them there is a level of inner chaos which results in an absence of any internal boundaries. Often home itself fails to provide any limits. Consequently, these children are unable to recognise any of the normal boundaries of behaviour proposed by school; they are too unhappy, angry or suffering from low self-esteem. Their only way to regain any feeling of personal power is to wind other children or adults up. Because of low self-esteem they do not believe they have the chance of being 'good', so don't even bother to try.

Mosley suggests that such children should be given 'tiny, attainable, tickable targets' (TATTS), which focus on particular aspects of their behaviour and reward them for achieving their target. These 'TATTS' may form the basis for specific behaviour contracts.

Mosley reminds us of the withdrawn child, who is also 'beyond' but is not disruptive and so can be easily overlooked. Such children, she says, have given up asking for their needs to be met. Mosley suggests specific strategies to involve such children in Circle Time, without forcing the child to speak (such as whispering their contribution to a puppet, with the teacher then speaking for the child to the whole group). The involvement of external agencies, such as child and family guidance, is suggested as needed for some of these children.

For children who do not make any significant improvement the stark reality of 'containment' is acknowledged, which should involve the development of an action plan by all members of staff in a school. It is emphasized that the child's teacher and classmates need support so that they are not adversely affected by such a child. Thus other members of staff and classes will need to share in the responsibility for this containment, until a suitable placement can be found. In relation to such a child Mosley (p. 43) says:

Other members of staff can offer practical support to allow 'time out' for either the child or the teacher. Supervised, practical tasks can be given to the child, e.g. sticking stamps on the school mail, helping the caretaker in simple jobs, or the child could spend some time working in another classroom. It is most important that the self-esteem of the teacher and other children is not drastically lowered by the child's behaviour.

What about the other children?

As the last quote indicates, what underscores some of the debate about the behaviour of certain children in school is the whole issue of the effect of their behaviour on other children. This issue was commonly cited in interviews with head teachers as one of the justifications for an exclusion. It is difficult to overemphasize the impact of a child 'beyond' on other children, although it is easier to argue why such children need to be with their peers. We will illustrate this debate with reference to one of the more extreme situations found during the field research. For example one behaviour support teacher described a child as a 'biter' who attacked other children. The child had been physically abused by his father who was a drinker. Two other children in his class had begun wetting the bed since his arrival in the class, and two others had become school refusers. The teacher said 'parents were queuing up wanting the child out of the school'. Apparently the behaviour support team was able to reduce the child's biting and began to substitute this behaviour for more acceptable behaviour. The child particularly liked a little girl who was encouraged to tell him that she did not like his biting behaviour, but she would allow him to stroke her hair or the back of her hand. Is this fair? we asked. In response the teacher said, 'other children are part of the healing process . . . they are coming from secure homes, where they are safe.'

Even supposing that this generalization applies to this little girl, it still needs to be considered whether children have the right *not* to help other children with their behaviour. It is worth reflecting for a moment, whether we as adults would feel amenable to a work colleague who had been physically aggressive, stroking our hands or hair, rather than hitting or biting us. On the other hand, if damaged children are not allowed to mix with well-adjusted pupils, where are they to learn appropriate behaviours?

As one primary head teacher said of the instances where she had been approached to take an excluded child whom other schools did not want to take: 'we know that if we won't take them, nobody else will . . . what's going to happen to them?' At the same time this head teacher was very conscious of the question of balance of intake to her school, in that if her school took on too many of the children other schools have excluded, 'that would destroy our delicate balance . . . We only just have enough ordinary kids to balance the others.' However, this primary school had a school council, which used Circle Time as part of their strategy to establish an ordered and caring environment. The head teacher believed in the capacity of other children to support others. This head teacher had instituted a system of 'Guardian Angels' who supported either the bullies or bullied children by intervening and helping to stop or divert behaviour, sometimes with the help of an adult. However, it was still acknowledged at this school that adults had to be seen to take action if a child became very aggressive. She described such an incident:

> A child suddenly attacked a lunchtime supervisor, causing a nasty injury. It shocked the other children. Other children had to see that he was punished. The child was involved in the decision, in fact the child's suggested punishment was a more severe and longer exclusion than we came up with. I think if it is negotiated [i.e. a fixed term exclusion], I do think it is useful. I think the children need to know that there may come a time in their lives when their behaviour will no longer be tolerated and that behaviour must be removed from the playground, if the child is unwilling to change it.

The behaviour policy of this school was clearly informed by both the Assertive Discipline and Circle Time approaches. A very important aspect of this school's policy is its relative simplicity and accessibility to children. Rules have been kept to the minimum and have been discussed and negotiated with the children. Time is set aside at the beginning of the school year to establish this framework and it is reinforced after every school holiday. Class rules are reinforced weekly at the beginning of Circle Time sessions, as well as via prominently displayed notices. Such policies can do a great deal to create a more caring, safe and predictable environment for children in school, but they will not prevent all exclusions. Yet they should provide a framework where fixed term exclusions are reduced and the ultimate sanction of permanent exclusion is avoided, or at least better managed. The power of whole-school policies could be considerably enhanced with the backing of other services in the form of complementary work with families.

Partnership with parents

Schools and parents have been encouraged to work together in partnership since 1967, when Plowden argued that this would bring greater understanding of pupils as well as support from home for school (Plowden Committee 1967). The Children Act 1989 has since given further impetus to the notion of working in partnership with parents (Buchanan 1994). While there are numerous schemes which attempt to involve and work with parents (for example, Moss 1992; Layzell 1995) there is still evidence of teachers' attitudes towards parents being negative, blaming home–school factors for pupils' behaviour (Layzell 1995). Forming genuine partnerships is likely to be difficult and involve criticism of schools and teachers, and thus the need to evaluate and adjust existing methods. Encouraging input, support and understanding for a school's behaviour management and disciplinary system from parents and carers, should provide two-way advantages for both home and school. However, partnerships may be particularly difficult to form with some of the parents/carers of children most at risk of exclusion, who have numerous moves and changes of adult carer. Effective partnerships for some children can only come about when schools and carers make extra effort in the attempt to forge the necessary contacts.

Lunchtimes and breaks

Children may spend between 20 and 25 per cent of their school day in breaks and lunchtimes. Problems between children can be initiated at these times and then spill over into class time. It is interesting to note that under the Children Act 1989, school age children up to 8 years should have one adult to eight children, while the recommended ratio is one adult to 12 children for over 8s, for activities outside the school day. Yet at lunchtimes in primary schools a ratio of one supervisor to 50 children is common (Stone and Dunton 1994: 30). Such individuals are not well paid and traditionally have not been trained. However, there is a growth in recognition of the importance of this time of the day as an opportunity for children who may not get the chance to play outside a great deal. Some of the GEST schemes have focused upon the training of lunchtime supervisors and have introduced a variety of constructive activities into this part of the school day (Learmonth 1995: 67). Some schools have put a great deal of effort into enhancing the quality of the playgrounds, providing environments which are both more bright and attractive and better organized for different types of activity which might otherwise cause conflict (see for example, Andrews and Hinton n.d.).

Summary and conclusions

This chapter has provided illustration of a range of education-based initiatives which address behaviour and may thus reduce exclusion. However, implicit in much of this chapter is a recognition that exclusion would be impossible to eliminate without a radical rethinking about how schools are organized and supported by other agencies as well as parents and carers. The availability of support to schools is limited in some localities. Ideally a range of levels of support are needed if certain children are to be kept in schools, in circumstances which are fair to all concerned. It is also clear that some schools do need help and support in developing their behaviour management and disciplinary systems.

There is a need for better inter-agency support and recognition of the realities of the variety of demands on a teacher (and children) in a class-room. In particular there is a need for the carers of children 'looked after' by social services departments to have a clear role (similar to that of the supportive parent) in relation to supporting the education of children in their care. Such children were heavily represented in the case studies in this research; as many observers, such as Jackson (1987) have said, they are children who have a great need for the opportunities that education might offer. There is also a need for a clear recognition that a range of services and provisions are necessary for children with emotional and behavioural dif-ficulties, if permanent exclusion from school is to be avoided. This range of services should include well-trained in-school classroom support, as well as individual counselling and therapy (see for example, Batmanghelidjh 1995); it may include internal exclusions on the school site (see for ex-ample, Dunn 1994); it may include part-time and short-term withdrawal to off-site centres; it should include special unit and school provision, as well as residential therapeutic environments. Education service-based initiatives should be able to reduce fixed term exclusions of primary age children. Better planning and support from other agencies involved with children at risk of permanent exclusion might help aid in their containment, until a suitable placement is found. Similar support and planning is necessary when such children are reintegrated into mainstream schools. In this way young children should be able to avoid the stigmatizing record of a permanent exclusion from school. Finally, as both Galloway *et al.* (1982) and Mosley (1993) have pointed out, there is a need to consider support for teachers faced with the stress of coping with unusually challenging children.

Nine

What can agencies outside the education service contribute?

Christine Sheppard

Background

The previous chapter has shown that, although a range of education service-based initiatives are being successfully deployed in schools, schools alone cannot solve the multifaceted problems of some children experiencing and manifesting behavioural difficulties. Firstly, schools need support from agencies outside the education service for pupils whose behaviour cannot be managed in the classroom no matter what strategy is employed. Schools may also have pupils who, although responsive to behaviour management strategies in the classroom, cannot maintain acceptable patterns of behaviour in situations where such external controls are absent, for example in the playground. In such cases appropriate interventions may be beyond the remit or professional training of teachers. Secondly, because some children may come from troubled home environments, in which positive behaviour patterns have not been internalized, parents need support if they are to fulfil the necessary task of supporting their children's education; parents in the case studies were reported to be calling for help with managing their children's behaviour at home. The need for parental support also applies to carers of children accommodated by social services, a high percentage of the case studies, who may not appreciate the important part which education can play in such children's lives, even though they act *in loco parentis*: Jackson (1987) highlighted the fact that education is not accorded a high priority in published guidelines for professionals in childcare practice.

However, while many of the families of excluded children studied already received services from outside agencies, predominantly from social services, other agency in-school initiatives for children having problems, or for parents needing support – either of which might help to prevent exclusion – were by no means routinely available. This is so despite evidence that school exclusion places increased demands on parents who may already be in difficulties and hence on social services departments, possibly even on the statutory child protection system (Bennathan 1992). While Webb (1994) calls for government funding to place social workers as a matter of course into schools serving deprived areas, the previous chapter has revealed that current LEA-run support services for those schools actually requesting help may be having to forego the vital input of even a part-time (social services) family worker to provide skilled parental support and a valuable home–school link, due to lack of available social services funding. The observation made two decades ago, that 'the different facets of a child's growth and development are so interdependent that they make nonsense of the division of our helping professions into separate – and often antagonistic – camps' (Fitzherbert 1977: 8), could equally well be made today. This issue undoubtedly affects the extent to which and ways in which agencies outside the education service are willing and/or able to contribute their expertise to tackle children's behaviour problems. However, while neither classroom nor parental support appears to be available routinely to schools, a number of promising, preventive initiatives addressing the home and school environments are to be found currently operating around the country.

Preventive initiatives

Current preventive work by agencies other than the education service can take a variety of forms. Utting *et al.* (1993) portrayed prevention as comprising three basic but overlapping approaches: services available to all, or 'universal' services; services sited in socially disadvantaged areas, or 'neighbourhood' services; and services targeted on individual children and their families known to be already experiencing severe problems, or 'preservation' services. This analysis has parallels with Durlak's (1995) three types of educational intervention, described in the introduction to Section 3. In social services terms (Hardiker *et al.* 1991), these three approaches would aim, respectively: to prevent the need arising for social services involvement; to intervene before problems become serious enough to require prolonged intervention; and to prevent children from being taken into care where problems have become acute. While all three approaches are necessary, it tends to be the latter, that is, crisis intervention, which is most prevalent; the universal service, the most truly preventive, is the least likely to be set up, due to its cost. It has been reported, for example, that the bulk of social services intervention is increasingly concerned with 'at risk' or emergency cases, with little possibility of use being made of Section 17 of the Children Act 1989 to support preventive work with children and families (Audit Commission 1994). Considerable evidence exists, however, to support the view that early intervention is more likely to prevent a young child's difficulties from developing into possibly intractable adolescent and/or adult problems (Rutter 1991; Farrington 1992; Rutter and Smith 1995). Longitudinal research studies, particularly those emanating from America, have confirmed this view that early, especially pre-school, interventions yield a wide range of long-term benefits, including better educational attainment, and are in fact more cost-effective (Berrueta-Clement *et al.* 1984; Schweinhart and Weikart 1993). There is also evidence that parents respond better to the non-stigmatizing nature of the universal service (Drake *et al.* 1995). The relationship of such initiatives to school exclusions is of course oblique, their aims being more explicitly concerned with family preservation and/or crime prevention. This, however, does not minimize their relevance to improved behaviour in schools and hence the incidence of exclusion.

In order to gain information about existing preventive initiatives for preschool and primary age children in Britain, a survey was conducted by the Social Services Research and Information Unit (SSRIU) of the University of Portsmouth during 1995. While by no means comprehensive, it has identified a wide variety of schemes, including: those conducted at national or local levels; those involving statutory, voluntary or charitable bodies; those with, or without, clear aims and theoretical approaches; and those running for a fixed term only, or indefinitely. Analysis of the data shows a marked tendency for mainstream services to work independently, siting their interventions within each of their disciplinary boundaries. Where inter-agency initiatives are taking place, they frequently focus on one arena and/or one actor only: the home (parenting skills), or the school (educational support for the child). The long-term effectiveness of such single-focus schemes has been called into question (Kazdin 1985), while more recent studies have stressed, in the context of preventing delinquency, the need for projects to encompass both the home and school environment (Graham and Bowling 1995). This is not to say, however, that relatively modest, single-agency and/or single-focus initiatives, which may not have the resources to mount more comprehensive schemes, cannot make an impact on their neighbourhoods.

Leaving aside all education service-based initiatives, responses to the survey included some of the more independent, yet relatively well-reported schemes, such as the American High/Scope Perry pre-school programme (Schweinhart and Weikart 1993), currently being piloted and evaluated in four UK sites by the Home Office, and 'The Place To Be', which provides individual psychotherapy and counselling in some London primary schools (Batmanghelidjh 1995). Moore *et al.* (1993) had found schools particularly receptive to the idea of individual counselling for children. By far the majority of responses to the survey, however, came from mainstream services and the major charities. These schemes generally have either a family-based or school-based focus. Within each of these two orientations, family or school, there are differences in size, scope and theoretical emphasis, but their similarities are more apparent than their differences: most significant is the fact that they tend to be social services driven. Two of the most typical types of scheme are described below. They were selected on the grounds that they have the potential to address the two specific non-education service areas identified in the previous chapter: the improvement of behaviour problems and the reduction of exclusion. The first type could be said to fall into Utting's second category, 'neighbourhood' services, while the second would more properly be termed a 'preservation' service (Utting *et al.* 1993), since such schemes generally deal with referred children and/or with children already in residential care.

Examples of preventive initiatives

Family support services

Although some family support schemes responding to the survey involve a variety of professionals, including health visitors and teachers, the more ubiquitous model seems to involve a partnership between a national charity – National Children's Homes' Action for Children, or Barnardo's – and a local social services department. Many such schemes are operating in inner-city areas or on large housing estates in family or community centres and may involve local residents in planning and operating the scheme. Typically, the staff team comprises a project leader, three or more project workers, a similar number of sessional workers running group activities or clubs, and parent helpers who may engage in direct work with children, or supply occasional administrative or domestic help.

The aims of family support schemes, invariably targeting both children and parents, are most often expressed in cognitive development rather than behavioural terms: for example, to provide activities related to social, physical and intellectual developmental needs of children; and to promote self-help skills, opportunities for self-development and social activities for parents. Parenting skills *per se* were specified in only one in five cases, although they may be implicitly provided in some of the other work.

The activities offered may include any or all of the following:

- a daily playgroup for the under-fives, in which parents are encouraged to become involved;
- a twice-weekly social club for school age children;
- a small group, two or three times weekly, having structured, individualized activities for children presenting a variety of problems (such as 'acting out' or withdrawn behaviour), referred by their parents and/or by social services;
- activities on a daily basis for children during school holidays;
- a daily 'drop-in' group for parents, providing the opportunity to discuss problems with a professional and, possibly, to engage in a parenting skills programme;
- a weekly parents' support group;
- home visits to individual families where requested.

Some respondents included supplementary material with their questionnaires which revealed that evaluation is largely confined to eliciting the perceptions of clients. The following representative extracts show that, though subjective, parents' comments nevertheless demonstrate the impact of schemes on a variety of problems:

> 'The playgroup gets them ready for full-time school and makes them more independent.'

> 'Before starting at the playgroup my son Billy was very shy and withdrawn and always played on his own. He's come on a lot . . . he's like a different little boy.'

> 'I enjoy coming to the playgroup because I see how they [staff] manage problems and that helps me with my own children at home.'

> 'I like talking to the other mums. You realize you're not the only one with problems.'

Family support schemes rely heavily on the drive, ideas, experience, expertise and commitment of the individual professionals and volunteers involved at a local level and so may be organized in very different ways. Compared to the comparatively well-established behaviour management strategies employed in the school setting and described in the previous chapter, they may appear to be relatively less focused since they do not have specific aims such as 'improving behaviour' and/or 'preventing exclusion'. Unlike most school-based strategies, however, they target pre-school children and parents, as well as school age children. Their main weaknesses appear to be that they may reach only a minority of disadvantaged families, that they can fail to involve fathers and minority ethnic families and that they are rarely objectively evaluated (Gibbons *et al.* 1990; Utting 1995; Smith and Pugh 1996). For the last reason they may not appear in the literature as frequently as the more specifically focused and rigorously evaluated education-based strategies. The Home Office, however, (Graham and Bowling 1995) is in no doubt of their value, believing the provision of such services, particularly parenting skills programmes, to be most important and calling for their extension to a national programme of universal parent education.

School-based support services

The purely education-based support services available to schools were found (in the research) to lack a complementary professional family input from social services departments (SSDs). The survey of preventive initiatives, however, identified the existence of SSD-run, school-based support services. Usually involving LEAs at the planning stage, they tend to be SSD-'owned' and funded and therefore joint initiatives only to the extent that they may have their funding 'topped up' by the LEA. Two main differences are immediately apparent between LEA and SSD-based in-school support services. Firstly, the latter usually attempt also to involve parents and carers of children accommodated by social services. Secondly, they tend to target individual children and their families or small groups rather than large groups, classes or a whole school. Social services in-school support differs from the above example of a typical family support service, although both are SSD-run, in that it takes place in schools, rather than in family or community centres; it also tends to be more behavioural than cognitive in theoretical orientation. Since the case studies reported in Section 2 comprised a high percentage of children accommodated or 'looked after' by social services, the following description represents the type of SSD in-school support scheme which caters specifically to such children.

The history of social services educational support for 'looked-after' children can be traced back to the demise of community homes with education (CHEs) within many local authorities during the 1980s and early 1990s. Among other reasons (such as cost), it came to be viewed as less disruptive to their education to support such children in their mainstream schools rather than to remove them to special CHE units for arbitrary periods of time (Hyland 1993). Some SSD education support services have since expanded to include children living in parental or foster homes who have been referred by their social workers. One of their common aims is to help to maintain children in school and, it follows, to prevent exclusion from school.

All team leaders responding to the survey indicated their willingness to supply further information. Some subsequently supplied quite detailed data. The following profile provides an indication of the circumstances of children served by one such scheme (Table 9.1) as well as its operational methods and timescales. The support service employs 16 caseworkers, most of whom are former CHE teachers. Workers have an average caseload of 24 children of all ages. Overall, 63 children are of primary school age (47 male, 16 female) representing just 16 per cent of the total number (385) of children, primary and secondary, having involvement with the support service at the time of the research. Those accommodated in children's homes are automatically referred upon entry; if their school performance is satisfactory, support workers will merely monitor progress. All other children have been individually referred by social workers as a result of their behavioural difficulties. For example, children living in the parental home may be referred to the education support service because they are on the brink of a care referral. Table 9.1 shows the accommodation and SEN circumstances of the 63 primary age children.

Table 9.1 shows that over one half (34, or 54 per cent) of these children have SEN statements, with a further seven (11 per cent) children having statements pending. The table also shows that by far the largest proportion of the statemented children (23, or 68 per cent) have been identified as having emotional and behavioural difficulties (EBD) and, furthermore, that such children are more likely to be resident in either the parental home or a children's home, suggesting that they may perhaps be difficult to place in a foster or adoptive home. Data provided by the team leader also reveal the

Table 9.1   Type of accommodation by existence of SEN statement during 1994

Special education need	Type of accommodation			Total	
	Children's home	Foster/project/ adoptive care	Parental home/ extended family	Nos.	%
EBD	11	1	11	23	37
Learning difficulty (MLD/SLD)	7	3	1	11	17
Statement pending	2	3	2	7	11
No SEN statement	6	3	13	22	35
Total	26 (41%)	10 (16%)	27 (43%)	63	100

Table 9.2   Permanent school exclusion by existence of SEN statement during 1994

Special education need	Permanent exclusion (still out of school)	Permanent exclusion (returned to education system)	No permanent exclusion	Total	
				Nos.	%
EBD	6	8	9	23	37
Learning difficulties (MLD/SLD)	1	1	9	11	17
Statement pending	1	0	6	7	11
No SEN statement	4	0	18	22	35
Total	12 (19%)	9 (14%)	42 (67%)	63	100

numbers and proportions of the 63 primary age children who have been permanently excluded from school. Table 9.2 matches these data to those on SEN statements.

Table 9.2 reveals that, of the 63 children, precisely one-third (21, or 33%) had received permanent exclusions, nine of whom had been found alternative schools while 12 were still out of school. Supplementary data show the average number of days spent out of school to be 146, ranging from 18 to 363 days. The table also suggests that children statemented for EBD are more likely to have been permanently excluded from school than are children diagnosed as experiencing learning difficulties, thus again upholding both the research evidence of Section 2 and the well-established findings of Galloway *et al.* (1982). Of the 12 children still out of school, six were reported to be receiving home tuition (to a maximum of five hours per person per week).

The high incidence of SEN statements and school exclusion amongst 'looked after' children and those known to SSDs, led to the creation of the SSD support service. The aims of the service are:

- to improve/maximize a child's educational experience and attainment, especially by raising the profile of education with children's home staff;
- to prevent school exclusion;
- to keep a child in the family home, i.e. to help prevent family breakdown (which can be precipitated by exclusion from school).

The type of support offered by support workers is varied and to a large extent left to the discretion of individual workers, particularly as they work mostly with individual children. Tasks for support workers were reported to include:

- providing educational visits;
- providing a 'role model' or 'authority figure';
- acting as an advocate for the child with the school;
- taking a refusing child to school in the mornings;
- sitting next to the child in 'difficult' lessons;
- talking about problems and ways to help the child address them;

and for excluded children only:

- giving children (educational) work to do, even though teaching is not part of the remit.

SSD education support services tend to be evaluated by local authority service quality departments. One such report made available had been jointly commissioned and carried out by the social services department and the education department. In summary, it recognized the valuable part played by the team in raising the profile of children's education with SSD staff within children's homes, and it approved the moves towards expanding services to provide much-needed support for foster parents. The SSD education support service's weaknesses were identified as a lack of clarity over support service roles and boundaries for both teachers and SSD field workers, leading to potential conflict; also poor communication with schools might lead to unrealistic expectations of the service. The report also stated that although the education support service was difficult to assess in terms of value for money due to its uniqueness and its highly qualitative outcomes, it should aim to collect data on costs, inputs, outputs and outcomes in order to inform judgements about the operation and effectiveness of the service in the future.

Agency conceptions and misconceptions

Both family support services and in-school support services identified from the survey had a strong social services bias. The latter service in particular, since it mostly operated within the school setting, might be expected to hold a very different conception of the problem of behaviour difficulty than an LEA-run educational support service as described in the previous chapter. The two agencies have been seen as being fundamentally incompatible at the personal and philosophical level. Normington (1994) holds that lengthy conflicts between social services departments and local education authorities are caused by differences in personality, training and perspective, while Roaf and Lloyd (1995) cite differences in professional culture, language, aims and priorities. Apparent incompatibility, however, may be more a consequence of professional cultures having developed in comparative isolation. Davie (1986), for example, regarded as 'astonishing' that education and social services, funded and controlled by the same authorities and dealing with the same children, even with the same problems, appear almost totally ignorant of each other's systems of assessment. Such a situation was certainly suggested by the report described above of an evaluation of one social services education support service: teachers' misconceptions had arisen regarding the support workers' role, which had given rise to some antagonism. All the more surprising then is the apparent similarity between the LEA-based and the SSD-based education support services. An examination of their procedures from the previous and present chapters reveals more similarities than differences. Perhaps for the reasons suggested above, however, the LEA-based service would appear to be more acceptable to schools at present. Better communication may facilitate the SSD support worker's role in schools.

Alternative conceptions

High numbers of children statemented for EBD were present in both the case studies and in the data provided by the SSD education support service. Many of these children were also found to be accommodated by the local authority. The case studies revealed that two-thirds (25 of the 38) children were in receipt of social services involvement and that almost one-half (17 of the 38) had spent time in the care of the local authority. They also served to illustrate the severity of some children's problems, for example physical violence towards other children, or actually running off the school premises. One inevitable consequence of the decision, however viewed, to close CHEs is the presence in mainstream schools of a greater number of such children, who need more attention than the average child in order to compensate for what the case studies also showed could be very disrupted lives. Schools, however, cannot provide the individual attention needed by young children who are so distressed. The research showed that education welfare officers too are unable to provide the necessary high level of care. The need for one-to-one support for some children was recognized in all three case study areas. It would seem therefore that social services education support services are particularly valuable in these circumstances, because they are organized in such a way that they can offer individual attention, advocate on behalf of the individual child, and provide a link between school and home (whether parental or local authority). They thus fulfil the task of supplying Utting's third ('preservation') service, which the education service or schools themselves are neither intended nor able to do. If comprehensive discussions and explanations were to take place at the level of the classroom teacher it is possible that teachers and SSD support workers would come to see their roles as complementary: that is, opposing conceptions and/or misconceptions may give way to alternative, positive conceptions of each agency's contribution to the problem of behavioural difficulty and school exclusion.

In a similar way, as has been suggested earlier, family support services at present fulfil the task of supplying Utting's second ('neighbourhood') type of service, in that they tend to be sited in areas of high socio-economic deprivation. Largely missing from the arena is Utting's first type of service, the 'universal', available to all and the most truly preventive service. The family support service model would seem to be particularly suitable for extension into a universal service, for the reason that it targets both very young children, pre-school as well as primary, and parents. The criticism that these services often fail to reach all needy families (and so certainly not all families) could, in theory at least, be solved by initiating their operation from primary school sites, thus making them potentially available to all parents/carers while having an input from schools. In this way the home–school link seen to be of crucial importance by the Home Office (Graham and Bowling 1995) and by established researchers in the field (for example, Wolfendale 1989) would be greatly facilitated.

Summary and conclusions

This chapter set out to examine ways in which agencies outside the education service can contribute to the amelioration of children's problem behaviour in and consequent exclusion from primary school. In particular it set out to look at the ways in which outside agencies can address the two specific areas of need identified in the previous chapter: in-school support and parental support. Drawing on a recent survey of currently operating preventive initiatives, two examples of typical schemes aiming to address each of these two foci were described. Each showed, albeit in different ways, benefits and problems, but above all they showed potential for broader application.

Children with behavioural problems are perhaps more traditionally seen as the concern of social services professionals, with teachers tending to view it as a social rather than an educational phenomenon and, as such, not really their concern. However sympathetic we may be to such a stance, it has become a fact of life that many teachers have to deal with difficult behaviour on a daily basis. If 'emotional and behavioural difficulty' could be accepted as another manifestation of 'learning difficulty' (it does after all inhibit learning), teachers might be more willing to accept that, as schools are unable to offer one-to-one attention to distressed children, social services are the obvious alternative to come on site to help. The chapter has also suggested that schools are the best site from which to run universal family support services. With the recent drive to make pre-school provision universal, the remaining issue appears to be the acknowledgement that inter-agency collaboration in primary schools may be the best way to promote the development of positive behaviour patterns and reduce the incidence of school exclusion.

Ten

Conclusions

Time spent in school is a central experience of childhood (Coleman 1992), next to the time spent with the family, for those who live at home. It is an obvious but nevertheless important point to make that children have to spend 40 weeks a year for over 11 years in school, a point highlighted by the study of Rutter *et al.* (1979). It is a period of time and experience which has enormous power to make us happy or miserable and to shape our view of ourselves (Jackson 1987, 1989). Attending school is not only about acquiring academic skills and knowledge, it is about learning to live with other people (Sylva 1994). Next to parents, teachers are, for the majority of children, the most influential people in their lives (Bennathan 1992). Bennathan (p. 6) comments how young people in trouble tend to remember teachers in their early days of school: 'often with affection, sometimes with bitterness, but certainly with great clarity as people who helped to shape their lives'.

Smith (1992) has also stressed 'the essential role' of education in enabling young people to prepare for the adult world and that children who do not have strong family support have to rely much more on success in education to support them in adulthood. There is evidence that many young people leaving care have a lack of academic attainments and that a large proportion go on to being unemployed and/or homeless (Jackson 1987; Smith 1992). Early parenthood is also a frequent occurrence for these young people. Furthermore, as Heath *et al.* (1994) have shown, foster care environments do not lead to an improvement in the educational prospects of children who may formerly have been placed in residential care. It is concluded that such children need more than average educational input to compensate for the situations they have experienced.

The interconnectedness of children who have major problems in school and those who are likely to go on to have major problems in other aspects of their adult lives, notably delinquent behaviour, is well documented (West and Farrington 1973; Reicher and Emler 1985). Yet, as these studies illustrate, the link is not inevitable: substantial numbers of pupils are delinquent but not disruptive in school and vice versa (Franklyn-Stokes 1989). Bennathan (1992) believes that as a society we show a lack of awareness about the nature of emotional and behavioural difficulties. She notes that with children we often assume that their troubles will pass and that they will forget, a prognosis about which she is not optimistic.

The need for additional, coordinated and appropriate support

Many of the children reported upon in Section 2 of this book need the support of a professional who is aware of both their home and school situation and is able to advocate with the relevant support agencies on behalf of that child. Education welfare officers are, perhaps, the most likely professional group to take on this advocacy role. However, this was not possible to any great extent in any of the case study LEAs in this research, both because of service level agreements which focused increasingly on their role in relation to school attendance and because of reductions in staffing. The need for this sort of support was recognized in all three of the case study LEAs, but their ability to provide it was partial and variable in each authority. Chapter 9 has suggested that social services educational support services may be well placed to fulfil a support role for the proportionally large group of 'looked-after' children at risk of exclusion from school.

The case studies illustrate that a range of levels of support are needed if certain children are to be kept in school. It is clear that some schools do need help and support in developing their behaviour management and disciplinary systems. Some case studies did suggest that already difficult situations could escalate because of the way they were managed by adults, particularly the cases which involved the physical restraint of children. Parents too could benefit from complementary systems of behaviour management and discipline in the home. Chapter 9 showed that valuable family support services do exist, but that they vary in specific focus and access and are usually sited in high priority areas; that is, they are not universal in nature. Schools as a mainstream service may have the potential for being both accessible and less stigmatizing venues for work on parenting skills than other establishments, such as social services-run family centres, child guidance clinics and psychiatric services. It is a potential which is utilized in some schools (Batmanghelidjh 1995), and some LEAs have systematically planned for these sorts of provision on the school site (see for example, Bowers 1995). However, it is a possibility which is often threatened in a period of reductions in public expenditure. Thus resources are an issue in a range of ways. Resources are often the underlying issue as to whether a child can be 'contained' within a school, and they certainly relate to whether the child gains access to more specialized help. Additional resources may be especially important for a child who is being reintegrated into mainstream schooling, after either a period in special education or out of school due to a permanent exclusion, or after major changes in home circumstances. In the research reported upon in Section 2 it was a happy circumstance if an adult was available, in a one-to-one situation, when they were needed by a child during the school day. The number and calibre of adults available during the school day in a primary school is critical. Staff absence or a head teacher off site attending a course or meeting can tip the balance to a situation where there is literally no additional adult available for a child. Depending on the level of difficulty or distress displayed by a child (and depending on the adults' interpretation of the situation) as well as the capacity of the class teacher (and others, including other children) to cope with it, a particular instance of 'unacceptable' behaviour might lead to an exclusion for a child. Social services in-school support services, with the remit to work one-to-one with a child, may contribute a valuable resource in such circumstances.

The future

In discussing the future shape of children's services, Jones and Bilton (1994: 5) put children centre stage, asking us to consider that:

> Children matter:
> as persons in their own right;
> as children with particular needs and rights;
> as the nation's future.

Clearly parents matter too, as Jones and Bilton go on to say. Like Young and Halsey (1995), they argue that parents should have the right to the support of the state and community in carrying the heavy and primary responsibility of bringing up children.

As with the research reported upon here, Jones and Bilton (1994) highlight the need for collaboration between services, most notably education, health and social services. Yet they also see the dividing up of responsibilities which has been accentuated by a market-orientated approach to service delivery. Professional values are viewed as often further accentuating the divisions between agencies. Local government reorganization is bringing both challenges as well as opportunities in the organization and delivery of children's services (Butler *et al.* 1995). Also, the Children Act 1989 attempts to promote a collaboration between services and professions in the interests of children 'in need'. Children's service plans build upon the requirements of the Children Act, with the aim of providing a comprehensive service for all children 'in need'. One of the groups of children identified as possibly benefiting from such plans is children excluded from school

(Sutton 1995). The latter part of the 1990s will begin to show whether these plans can deliver a better service to such children and their families. Such a service should be preventive in focus, rather than a better service after exclusion has occurred.

Primary age children excluded from school might be viewed as a particularly vulnerable group of children 'in need'. From the research evidence presented in this book they do indeed (as Bennathan 1992 has suggested) appear to be an extreme group in terms of the range and depth of their needs.

The evidence to date shows a continuing rise in the number of recorded exclusions, with developing education and other social policies doing very little to stop this trend. The survey conducted by Parsons *et al.* (1995), as well as that by the NAHT (1994), has been interpreted as evidence that the removal of the indefinite category of exclusion in September 1994 may have led to a further increase in permanent exclusions. However, Parsons' (1995) estimate for the whole of the 1994–5 academic year shows an easing off in the records of permanent exclusion. Nevertheless, the first half of the 1990s has shown a more than fourfold increase in records of permanent exclusion from school. The Education Act 1993 and the 'Pupils with problems' circulars (DfE 1994a) confirm the place of exclusion in the disciplinary armoury of schools. The DfE advice with regard to exclusion concentrates as much on appropriate procedure and provision as on prevention. The expectation that LEAs will set up pupil referral units is a confirmation that exclusion and segregation of some children is likely to continue. The continuing pressure to produce better academic results, to make these results public and to increase the number of grant maintained schools is unlikely to work in favour of the kind of children reported upon in this research. Furthermore, the lack of additional funding for the implementation of the Code of Practice (Dyer 1995), in relation to special educational needs, leaves children with EBD very vulnerable when decisions are made about the allocation of already inadequate resources. The reductions in resources available to schools in the 1995–6 academic year in many LEAs, further exacerbate the situation.

Blyth and Milner (1996) are optimistic about the ability of quasi-markets to cater differently for secondary age pupils, particularly the majority of excluded children who are in their last two years of compulsory schooling. However, such provision by its very nature may be inappropriate for primary age children. That is, if they are put on programmes which disapply them from following the National Curriculum, their chances of reintegration to mainstream education at a later date will be greatly reduced. On the other hand, alternative programmes for younger children could focus more on supported reintegration into school after a period outside it. There is evidence that this is beginning to happen with organizations like Cities in Schools and in certain pupil referral units. Primary school children who are excluded from school are a tiny minority of all school children. We can decide through the way social policy is interpreted, adapted and reformulated whether we ignore this minority or plan and cater for it appropriately. If we choose to ignore it we will still have to reap the effects of crises precipitated by ignoring such obvious need; if we try to make appropriate provision we may reap the rewards of some successes, as well as avert some crises.

A growing awareness of the financial, as well as the social costs, of crisis intervention (Parsons 1994) in cases of school exclusion may be fostered by a market-orientated, budget-conscious system of service delivery. As one LEA official in this research pointed out, the gap in resource terms between a few extra hours support from an SNA (at about £6 an hour) and the cost of an out-of-county placement (at upwards of £45,000 a year) is enormous. There could be, should be (and sometimes there are) other alternatives to permanent exclusion from primary school, even within the current financial constraints. However, such alternatives may well involve services and professionals rethinking their roles and responsibilities. In LEA 3 this step had already been taken, with one service (an external provider and charitable organization, Cities in Schools) taking the key coordinating responsibility for children and their families when a primary age child was excluded from school permanently. Such a move was only possible through the closure of part of the LEA service and the attendant redundancies of staff. It is too early to assess whether such a move will provide a better service for children and their families. Politically it is a decision which angers many committed public service employees; it also divides those who view as urgent the need for changes in the way services are delivered to vulnerable children.

Bibliography

Advisory Centre for Education (ACE) (1991) Exclusion from school, *ACE Bulletin*, 41: 7–12.

ACE (1992) Exclusions, *ACE Bulletin*, 45: 9–10.

ACE (1993a) *Children out of School: a Guide for Parents and Schools on Non-Attendance at School*. London: ACE.

ACE (1993b) *Findings from ACE Investigations into Exclusions*. London: ACE.

Andrews, C. and Hinton, S. (n.d.) *Enhancing the Quality of School Playgrounds*, a Pilot Project. London: The National Children's Play and Recreation Unit.

Association of Educational Psychologists (AEP) (1992) Press release on exclusions survey, 23 April.

Association of Metropolitan Authorities (AMA) (1995) Special Needs, press release 26 January, ref. 6/95.

Audit Commission (1994) *Seen but not heard; Coordinating Community Child Health and Social Services for Children in Need*. London: HMSO.

Badger, B. (1985) Behavioural problems – the primary-secondary link, *School Organization*, 5(2): 185–93.

Ball, S. (1993) Education policy, power relations and teacher's work, *British Journal of Educational Studies*, 41(2): 106–21.

Barker, P. (1993) The child in the chaotic family, in V. Varma (ed.) *How and Why Children Fail*, pp. 103–13. London: Jessica Kingsley.

Barrett, G. (1989) *Disaffection from School? The Early Years*. Lewes: The Falmer Press.

Bartlett, W. (1992) Quasi-markets and educational reforms: a case study, *Studies in Decentralisation and Quasi-Markets*. Bristol: SAUS.

Batmanghelidjh, C. (1995) Supporting children in primary school, *Young Minds Newsletter*, 22: 12–13.

Beckett, F. (1992) Law unto itself ? *Education*, 180(7): 127.

Bennathan, M. (1992) The care and education of troubled children, *Therapeutic Care and Education*, 10(1): 1–7.

Berrueta-Clement, J. R., Schweinhart, L. J., Barnett, W. S., Epstein, A. S. and Weikart, D. P. (eds) (1984) *Changed Lives: the Effects of the Perry Preschool Program on Youth Through Age 19*. Ypsilanti, MI: High Scope.

Blenkin, G. and Kelly, V. (1994) The death of infancy, *Education 3–13*, 22(3): 3–9.

Blyth, E. and Milner, J. (1993) Exclusion from school: a first step in exclusion from society? *Children and Society*, 7(3): 255–68.

Blyth, E. and Milner, J. (1994) Exclusion from school and victim blaming, *Oxford Review of Education*, 20(3): 293–306.

Blyth, E. and Milner, J. (1996) Unsaleable goods and the education market, in C. Pole and R. Charla-Duggan (eds) *Reshaping Education in the 1990s: Perspectives on Secondary Schooling*. London: Falmer Press.

Bourne, J., Bridges, L. and Searle, C. (1994) *Outcast England – How Schools Exclude Black Children*. London: Institute of Race Relations.

Bowers, M. (1995) White City child guidance unit, *Young Minds Newsletter*, 20: 16–17.

British Broadcasting Corporation (BBC) (1993) *Panorama*: 'A class apart', 15 March.

BBC (1994) *First Sight*: 'The ex generation', 10 November.

Bryan, J. and Simpson, A. (1995) *BST [Behaviour Support Team] Teacher Information*. Devon South Behaviour Support Team.

Buchanan, A. (ed.) (1994) *Partnership in Practice. The Children Act 1989*. Aldershot: Avebury.

Butler, I., Davies, M. and Noyes, P. (1995) *Planning for Children. The Effects of Local Government Reorganisation*. NSPCC: Cardiff and London.

Canter, L. and Canter, M. (1992) *Assertive Discipline*. Bristol: Behaviour Management Ltd.

Carlen, P., Gleeson, D. and Wardhaugh, J. (1992) *Truancy: the Politics of Compulsory Schooling*. Buckingham: Open University Press.

Carroll, J. (1995) Reaching out to aggressive children, *The British Journal of Social Work*, 25(1): 37–53.

Chandler, L. (1981) The source of stress inventory, *Psychology in the Schools*, 18: 164–8.

Chandler, L. (1985) *Assessing Stress in Children*. New York: Praegar.

Chandler, L., Shermis, M. D. and Marsh, J. (1985) The use of the stress response scale in diagnostic assessment with children, *Journal of Psychoeducational Assessment*, 3: 15–29.

Channel 4 (1993) *Free for All*, 2 March.

Cicourel, A. V. and Kitsuse, J. I. (1963) *The Educational Decision-Makers*. Indiana, USA: Bobbs-Merrill.

Cohen, R. (1994) Outside looking in, *Community Care*, 1047: 24–5.

Cohen, R., Hughes, M., with Ashworth, L. and Blair, M. (1994) *School's Out*. Ilford: Family Service Units/Barnado's.

Cohen, S. (1980) *Folk Devils and Moral Panics*. Oxford: Martin Robertson.

Coleman, J. C. (ed.) (1992) *The School Years. Current Issues in the Socialisation of Young People*, Second edition. London and New York: Routledge.

Conduct Problems Prevention Research Group (CPPRG) (1992) A developmental and clinical model for the prevention of conduct disorder: the FAST Track program, *Development and Psychopathology*, 4: 509–27.

Cooper, P. (1994a) Attention deficit hyperactivity disorder and the strange case of Vincent Van Gogh, *Therapeutic Care and Education*, 3(2): 86–95.

Cooper, P. (1994b) Effective responses to emotional and behavioural difficulties. Paper presented to National Children's Bureau Conference: Children with Emotional and Behavioural Difficulties, London, 8 December.

Copeland, I. C. (1994) Exclusion from school: the agenda and the players, *Education Today*, 44(4): 13–20.

Coxon, P. (1988) A primary approach to misbehaviour, *Special Children*, 24 (October): 22–3.

Davie, R. (1986) Understanding behaviour problems, *Maladjustment and Therapeutic Education*, 4(1): 2–11.

Davie, R. (1994) A consortium for children: analysis of a dialogue with policy-makers leading to the 1993 Education Act and the 1994 Code of Practice, *Therapeutic Care and Education*, 3(3): 206–17.

Department for Cultural Studies (DCS), University of Birmingham (1981) *Unpopular Education. Schooling and Social Democracy in England since 1944*. London: Hutchinson.

DCS (1991) *Education Limited. Schooling and Training and the New Right since 1979*. London: Unwin Hyman.

Department of Education and Science and the Welsh Office (DES/WO) (1989) *Discipline in Schools. Report of the Committee of Inquiry Chaired by Lord Elton*. London: HMSO.

Department for Education (DfE) (1992) *Exclusions – a Discussion Paper*. London: DfE.

DfE (1994a) *Pupils with Problems*, circulars 8–13/94: 8/94, Pupil behaviour and discipline; 9/94, The education of children with emotional and behavioural diffi culties; 10/94, Exclusions from school, 11/94, The education by LEAs of children otherwise than at school; 12/94, The education of sick children; 13/94, The education of children looked after by local authorities. London: DfE.

DfE (1994b) *Code of Practice on the Identification and Assessment of Special Educational Needs*. London: DfE.

DfE (1995) *Education Facts and Figures, England*. London: DfE.

DFEE (1995) Grants for Education Support and Training (GEST) scheme. Truancy and disaffected pupils category. *Directory of Approved Projects 1994–95*. London: DFEE.

Department of Health and Office for Standards in Education (DoH/OFSTED) (1995) *The Education of Children who are Looked after by Local Authorities*. London: HMSO.

Drake, B., Berfield, M., D'Gama, L. A., Gallagher, J. P., Gibbs, M., Henry, S. and Lin, D. (1995) Implementing the family preservation program: feedback from focus groups with consumers and providers of services, *Child and Adolescent Social Work Journal*, 12(5): 391–410.

Dunn, P. (1994) Through the mill and back again, *Times Educational Supplement*, 30 December: 24.

Durlak, J. A. (1995) *School-based Prevention Programmes for Children and Adolescents*. Vol. 34, Developmental Clinical Psychology and Psychiatry. London: Sage.

Dyer, C. (1995) The Code of Practice through LEA eyes, *British Journal of Special Education*, 22(2): 48–51.

Education (1993a) Forth predicts return to expulsion, *Education*, 182(3): 44.

Education (1993b) Behaviour unchanged but exclusions rise, *Education*, 182(25): 454.

Edwards, T. and Whitty, G. (1992) Parental choice and educational reform in Britain and the United States, *British Journal of Educational Studies*, 40(2): 101–17.

Farrington, D. (1980) Truancy, delinquency, the home and the school, in L. Hersov and I. Berg (eds) *Out of School: Modern Perspectives on Truancy and School Refusal*. Chichester: John Wiley.

Farrington, D. (1992) Criminal career research in the United Kingdom, *British Journal of Criminology*, 32(4): 521–36.

Field, F. (1990) Britain's underclass: countering the growth, in C. Murray *The Emerging British Underclass*. Choice in Welfare Series No. 2. London: The IEA Health and Welfare Unit.

Fitzherbert, K. (1977) *Child Care Services and the Teacher*. London: Temple Smith.

Fox, G. (1995) *The 'Inclusion' Project*. Autumn 1994–March 1995. Southampton: Hampshire Educational Psychology Service.

Franklyn-Stokes, B. A. (1989) 'Suspension from school: Who? Why? and with what consequences?' PhD submitted to the Department of Psychology, University of Bristol.

Furlong, V. J. (1985) *The Deviant Pupil: Sociological Perspectives*. Milton Keynes: Open University Press.

Gale, I. and Topping, K. (1986) Suspension from high school: the practice and its effects, *Pastoral Care in Education*, 4(3): 215–24.

Galloway, D. (1985) Persistent absence and exclusion from school: the predictive power of school and community variables, *British Educational Research Journal*, 11(1): 51–61.

Galloway, D., Ball, T., Blomfield, D. and Seyd, R. (1982) *Schools and Disruptive Pupils*. London: Longman.

Garmezy, N. (1981) Children under stress: perspectives on antecedents and correlates of vulnerability and resistance to psychopathology, in A. I. Rabin *et al.* (eds) *Further Explorations in Personality*. New York: Wiley.

Garner, P. (1993) Exclusions: the challenge to schools, *Support for Learning*, 8(3): 99–103.

Gersch, I. S. and Nolan, A. (1994) Exclusions: what the children think, *Educational Psychology in Practice*, 10(1): 35–45.

Gibbons, J. with Thorpe, S. and Wilkinson, P. (1990) *Family Support and Prevention*. London: National Institute for Social Work/HMSO.

Gibson, D. (1994) Exclusions from school: bridging the gap between policy and practice, *Therapeutic Care and Education*, 3(1): 72–5.

Gillborn, D. (1995) Racism and exclusions from school – case studies in the denial of educational opportunity. Paper presented at the European Conference on Educational Research (ECER 95), University of Bath, 14–17 September.

Goldstein, S. (1994) Understanding and assessing ADHD and related educational, behavioural and emotional disorders, *Therapeutic Care and Education*, 3(2): 111–29.

Graham, J. H. (1988) *Schools, Disruptive Behaviour and Delinquency*. Home Office Research Study No. 96. London: HMSO.

Graham, J. and Bowling, B. (1995) *Young People and Crime*. Home Office Research Study No. 145. London: HMSO.

Graham, J. and Smith, D. I. (1993) *Diversion from Offending: the Role of the Youth Service*. London: Crime Concern.

Green, D. G. (1987) *The New Right. The Counter Revolution in Political, Economic and Social Thought*. London: Harvester Wheatsheaf.

Grimshaw, R. and Berridge, D. (1994) *Educating Disruptive Children*. London: National Children's Bureau.

Grunsell, R. (1979) *Beyond Control? Schools and Suspension*. London: Writers and Readers.

Hall, C. (1995) 'Stress' pushing up school exclusions, *The Independent*, 4 April: 7.

Halsey, A. H. (1993) Changes in the family, *Children and Society*, 7(2): 125–43.

Hankin, J. (1993) Child and family mental health services: the struggle continues, *Young Minds Newsletter*, 16: 2–4.

Hanko, G. (1994) Discouraged children: when praise does not help, *British Journal of Special Education*, 21(4): 166–8.

Hardiker, P., Exton, K. and Barker, M. (1991) *Policies and Practices in Preventative Child Care*. Aldershot: Avebury.

Hargreaves, D., Hester, S. K. and Mellor, F. J. (1975) *Deviance in Classrooms*. London: Routledge and Kegan Paul.

Havas, E. (1995) The family as ideology, *Social Policy and Administration*, 29(1): 1–9.

Hayden, C. (1994) Primary age children excluded from school: a multi-agency focus for concern, *Children and Society*, 8(3): 132–48.

Hayden, C. (1996) Primary school exclusions: the need for integrated solutions, in E. Blyth and J. Milner (eds) *Exclusion from School: Inter-professional Issues in Policy and Practice*. London: Routledge.

Hayden, C., Sheppard, C. and Ward, D. (1996) Primary exclusions: evidence for action, *Research in Education*, 38(2): 1–13.

Heath, A. F., Colton, M. J. and Aldgate, J. (1994) Failure to escape: a longitudinal study of foster children's educational attainment, *British Journal of Social Work*, 24: 241–260.

Herbert, M. (1985) Family-orientated behaviour work, *Maladjustment and Therapeutic Education*, 4(2): 67–73.

Hofkins, D. (1994) Expulsions rocket to double 1991, *Times Educational Supplement*, 28 October, 4087: 2.

Holdsworth, N. (1995) Excluded children in care 'a scandal', *Times Educational Supplement*, 7 July, 4123: 5.

Hyland, J. (1993) *Yesterday's Answers: Development and Decline of Schools for Young Offenders*. London: Whiting and Birch/SCA.

Ideus, K. (1994) Cultural foundations of ADHD: a sociological analysis, *Therapeutic Care and Education*, 3(2): 173–94.

Imich, A. J. (1994) Exclusions from school: current trends and issues, *Educational Research*, 36(1): 3–11.

Jackson, S. (1987) *The Education of Children in Care*. Bristol Papers. Bristol: SAUS.

Jackson, S. (1989) Residential care and education, *Children and Society*, 4: 335–50.

Jones, A. and Bilton, R. (1994) *The Future Shape of Children's Services*. London: National Children's Bureau.

Kazdin, A. E. (1985) *Treatment of Anti-Social Behaviour in Children and Adolescents*. Homewood, IL: Dorsey.

Kurtz, Z., Thornes, R. and Wolkind, S. (1994) *Services for the Mental Health of Children and Young People in England – a National Review*. London: Maudsley Hospital and South Thames (West) Regional Health Authority.

Labov, W. (1973) The logic of nonstandard English, in N. Keddie (ed.) (1973) *Tinker, Tailor?* Harmondsworth: Penguin.

Lamb, P. (1993) *Exclusions from Islington Schools 1991–92*. London: Islington Education Department.

Laslett, R. (1983) *Changing Perceptions of Maladjusted Children*. Portishead: AWMC.

Lawrence, J. and Steed, D. (1986) Primary school perception of misbehaviour, *Educational Studies*, 12(2): 147–56.

Lawrence, J., Steed, D. and Young, P. (1984) *Disruptive Children: Disruptive Schools?* Orpington: Croom Helm.

Layzell, P. (1995) A case study of a parental involvement scheme, *Therapeutic Care and Education*, 4(2): 30–5.

Learmonth, J. (1995) *More Willing to School? An Independent Evaluation of the Truancy and Disaffected Pupils GEST Programme*. London: DfEE.

Le Grand, J. and Bartlett, W. (1993) *Quasi-Markets and Social Policy*. Basingstoke: Macmillan.

Levačić, R. (1994) Evaluating the performance of quasi-markets in education, in W. Bartlett *et al. Quasi-Markets in the Welfare State*. Bristol: SAUS.

Lineham, T. (1994) School's out *Community Care*, 999: 7.

Lloyd Bennett, P. (1995) Bringing it home, *Education*, 185(22): 13.

Lloyd-Smith, M. (1984) *Disrupted Schooling. The Growth of the Special Unit*. London: John Murray.

Lloyd-Smith, N. (1993) Problem behaviour, exclusions and the policy vacuum, *Pastoral Care in Education*, 11(4): 19–24.

Lockwood, D. (1985) 'Civic exclusion', mimeo, University of Essex.

Lovey, J., Docking, J. and Evans, R. (1993) *Exclusion from School: Provision for Disaffection at Key Stage 4*. London: David Fulton in association with Roehampton Institute.

Lowenstein, L. F. (1990) Dealing with the problem of expelled pupils, *Education Today*, 40(4): 35–7.

Maginnis, E. (1993) An inter-agency response to children with special needs – the Lothian experience (a Scottish perspective). Paper presented to National Children's Bureau Conference, Exclusions from School: Bridging the Gap between Policy and Practice, 13 July.

Malek, M. (1993) *Passing the Buck*. London: The Children's Society.

Marks, D. (1995) Accounting for exclusion: giving a 'voice' and producing a 'subject', *Children and Society*, 9(3): 81–98.

Mayet, G. (1992) What hope for children with learning and behavioural difficulties? *Concern*, 82: 3.

McLean, A. (1987) After the belt: school processes in low-exclusion schools, *School Organization*, 7(3): 303–10.

McManus, M. (1987) Suspension and exclusion from high schools: the association with catchment and school variables, *School Organization*, 7(3): 261–71.

McManus, M. (1989) *Troublesome Behaviour in the Classroom: a Teachers' Survival Guide*. London: Routledge.

McVicar, M. (1991) Education policy: education as a business?, in S. Savage and L. Robins (eds) *Public Policy Under Thatcher*. pp. 131–44. Basingstoke: Macmillan Education.

Mihill, C. (1995) Pupils 'expelled to impress parents', *Guardian*, 4 April: 3.

Mittler, J. (1995) Special needs education: an international perspective. *British Journal of Special Education*, 22(3): 105–8.

Moore, D., Decker, S., Greenwood, A. and Kirby, S. (1993) Research into the demand for counselling/therapeutic provision in a group of primary schools, *Educational Research*, 35(3): 276–81.

MORI (1993) *Exclusions and Education Resourcing*. Report prepared for BBC Panorama. London: MORI.

Mortimore, P., Sammons, P., Stoll, L., Lewis, D. and Echo, K. (1988) *School Matters: the Junior Years*. Wells: Open Books.

Mosley, J. (1993) *Turn Your School Round*. Wisbech: LDA.

Moss, P. (1992) The Oxfordshire movement, *Education*, 179(19): 376–7.

Murray, C. (1990) *The Emerging British Underclass*. Choice in Welfare Unit No. 2. London: IEA Health and Welfare Unit.

National Association of Head Teachers (NAHT) (1994) Press release: Dramatic increase in permanent exclusions of pupils, 9 December.

National Commission on Education (NCE) (1993) *Special Needs Education: the Next 25 Years*. NCE Briefing 14. London: NCE.

NCE (1995) *Standards in Literacy and Numeracy: 1948–1994*. NCE Briefing 7. London: NCE.

Normington, J. (1994) Exclusion from school; the role of outside agencies. Paper presented to conference, Behaviour Problems in Schools and Exclusion: Education and Social Work Responses, University of Huddersfield, Centre for Education Welfare Studies, 14–15 July.

Nottingham County Council Education Department (NCCED) (1989) *Pupil Exclusions from Nottingham Secondary Schools*. Advisory and Inspection Service. Report No. 15189. Nottingham: County Council Education Department.

NUT (1992) *Survey on Pupil Exclusions*. London: National Union of Teachers.

OECD (1994) *School – a Matter of Choice?* Paris: OECD.

Office for Standards in Education (OFSTED) (1993) *Education for Disaffected Pupils*. London: OFSTED.

OFSTED (1995) *Pupil Referral Units. The First Twelve Inspections*. London: OFSTED.

O'Keeffe, D. (1994) *Truancy in English Secondary Schools*. London: HMSO.

Parffrey, V. (1990) An alternative to exclusion from school: the Tor Hill project, *Educational Psychology in Practice*, 5(4): 216–21.

Parsons, C. (1994) The cost of primary school exclusions. Paper presented to conference, Behaviour Problems in School and Exclusion: Education and Social Work Responses, University of Huddersfield, Centre for Education Welfare Studies, 14–15 July.

Parsons, C. (1995) Permanent exclusions: the present situation, trends, causes and responses. Paper presented to conference, The Prevention and Management of Exclusion from School. An Inter-agency Conference, University of York, 6 October.

Parsons, C., Benns, L., Hailes, J. and Howlett, K. (1994) *Excluding Primary School Children*. London: Family Policy Studies Centre/Joseph Rowntree Foundation.

Parsons, C., Hailes, J., Howlett, K., Davies, A. and Driscoll, P. (1995) *National Survey of Local Education Authorities' Policies and Procedures for the Identification of, and Provision for, Children who are out of School by Reason of Exclusion or Otherwise*. London: DfE.

Peagram, E. (1991) Swings and roundabouts: aspects of statementing and provision for children with emotional and behavioural difficulties, *Maladjustment and Therapeutic Education*, 9(3): 160–8.

Peagram, E. (1993) 'The incidence and nature of and the response of an LEA to, serious emotional and behavioural disturbance among primary school children'. PhD thesis submitted to the School of Education, University of Birmingham.

Peagram, S. (1995) The foolish man built his house on sand, *Therapeutic Care and Education*, 4(1): 9–16.

Pisano, S. (1991) Children with emotional and behavioural difficulties in the primary school, *Maladjustment and Therapeutic Education*, 9(3): 170–3.

Plowden Committee (1967) *Children and their Primary Schools* [The Plowden Report]. London: HMSO.

Pyke, N. (1993) Police fear a rising tide of exclusions, *Times Educational Supplement*, 4038: 1.

Pyke, N. (1995) Inspections 'neglect' racial equality, *Times Educational Supplement*, 3 February, 4101: 5.

Quamma, J. P. and Greenburg, M. T. (1994) Children's experience of life stress: the role of social support and social problem-solving skills as protective factors, *Journal of Clinical Child Psychology*, 23(3): 295–305.

Reicher, S. and Emler, N. (1985) Delinquent behaviour and attitudes to formal authority, *British Journal of Social Psychology*, 24: 161–8.

Reid, J. (1987) A problem in the family: explanations under strain, in T. Booth and D. Coulby (eds) *Producing and Reducing Disaffection*. Milton Keynes: Open University Press.

Reynolds, D., Jones, D. and St Ledger, S. (1976) Schools do make a difference, *New Society*, 37(271): 223–5.

Roaf, C. and Lloyd, C. (1995) *Multi-Agency Work with Young People in Difficulty*. Oxford: Oxford Brookes University/Joseph Rowntree Foundation

Robotham, D. (1995) Searching for the truth, *Education*, 186(10): 17–18.

Rogers, R. (1993) *A Guide to the Education Act 1993. An ACE Handbook*. London: The Advisory Centre for Education.

Rollinson, S. (1990) Being nice to nasties, *Special Children*, 37: 7–9.

Ronen, T. (1993) Adapting treatment techniques to children's needs, *British Journal of Social Work*, 23(6): 581–96.

Rutter, M. (1978) Family, area and school influence in the genesis of conduct disorders, in L. Hersov, M. Berger and D. Schaffer (eds) *Aggression and Anti-social Behaviour in Childhood and Adolescence*. Oxford: Pergamon.

Rutter, M. (1981) Stress, coping and development: some issues and some questions, *Journal of Child Psychology and Psychiatry*, 22(4): 323–56.

Rutter, M. (1991) Services for children with emotional disorders, *Young Minds Newsletter*, 9 October.

Rutter, M., Cox, A., Tupling, C., Berger, M. and Yule, W. (1975) Attainment and adjustment in two geographical areas: the prevalence of psychiatric disorder, *British Journal of Psychiatry*, 126: 493–509.

Rutter, M., Maughan, B., Mortimore, P. and Custon, J. (1979) *Fifteen Thousand Hours: Secondary Schools and their Effects on Pupils*. London: Open Books.

Rutter, M. and Smith, D. J. (eds) (1995) *Psychosocial Disorders in Young People. Time Trends and Their Causes*. Published for Academis Europaea. Chichester: John Wiley.

Rutter, M., Tizard, J. and Whitmore, K. (1970) *Education, Health and Behaviour*. London: Longman.

Sasson, D. (1992) An odd state of affairs, *Education*, 180(4): 92.

Sasson, D. (1993) The price of banishment, *Education*, 181(6): 111.

Schweinhart, L. J. and Weikart, D. (1993) *A Summary of Significant Benefits: the High/Scope Perry Pre-school Study Through Age 27*. Ypsilanti, MI: High/Scope Press.

Secondary Heads Association (SHA) (1992) *Excluded from School: a Survey of Suspensions from Secondary Schools in 1991–92*. Leicester: SHA.

Sinclair, R., Grimshaw, R. and Garnett, L. (1994) The education of children in need: the impact of the Education Reform Act 1988, the Education Act 1993 and the Children Act 1989, *Oxford Review of Education*, 20(3): 281–92.

Smith, C. and Pugh, G. (1996) *Learning to be a Parent: a Survey of Group-based Parenting Programmes*. London: Family Policy Studies Centre (for the Joseph Rowntree Foundation).

Smith, P. (1992) Is there life after care?, *Concern*, 82: 8–9.

Special Educational Consortium (1993) *Response by the Special Educational Consortium and the National Children's Bureau to the Consultation by the Department for Education on Exclusions*. London: Council for Disabled Children and National Children's Bureau.

Steinhauer, P. D., Santa-Barbara, J. and Skinner, H. (1984) The process model of family functioning, *Canadian Journal of Psychiatry*, 29: 77–97.

Stirling, M. (1991) The exclusion zone, *Managing Schools Today*, 1(3): 8–10.

Stirling, M. (1992) The Education Reform Act and EBD children, *ACE Bulletin*, 45: 7–8.

Stirling, M. (1993a) Second classes for a second class?, *Special Children*, 66: 15–18.

Stirling, M. (1993b) A 'black mark' against him? Why are African-Caribbean boys over-represented in the excluded pupil population? *Multicultural Education Review*, 15: 3–6.

Stone, L. and Dunton, G. (1994) Playing fair, *Managing Schools Today*, 3(7): 30–1.

Sutton, P. (1995) *Crossing the Boundaries*. London: National Children's Bureau.

Sylva, K. (1994) School influences on children's development, *Journal of Child Psychology and Psychiatry*, 35(1): 135–70.

Taylor, F. (1992) The ins and outs, *Times Educational Supplement*, 27 November: G27.

Taylor, P. (1992) Understanding exclusion, *Education*, 180(6): 115.

Times Educational Supplement (TES) (1991) Excluding a stitch at a time, 3 May, 3905: 13.

Tutt, N. (1983) Maladjustment – a sociological perspective, *Maladjustment and Therapeutic Education*, 1(2): 7–24.

Upton, G. (1981) The nature and development of behaviour problems, in G. Upton and A. Gobell (eds) *Behaviour Problems in the Comprehensive School*. Cardiff: Faculty of Education, University College.

Utting, D. (1995) *Family and Parenthood: Supporting Families, Preventing Breakdown*. York: Joseph Rowntree Foundation.

Utting, D., Bright, J. and Henricson, C. (1993) *Crime and the Family*. Occasional Paper 16. London: Family Policy Studies Centre.

Veljanovski, C. (1990) Foreword, to A. De Jaysay, *Market Socialism: a Scrutiny of 'The Square Circle'* p. 6. London: Institute of Economic Affairs.

Ward, D. (1994) 'Basic' Patten list baffles head whose tough rules already work, *Guardian*, 5 January: 2.

Warnock, H. M. (Chair) (1978) 'Special educational needs', *Report of the Committee of Inquiry into the Education of Handicapped Children and Young People*. London: HMSO.

Webb, R. (1994) *After the Deluge: Changing roles and responsibilities in the primary school*. London: ATL.

Wedell, K. (1995) Making inclusive education ordinary, *British Journal of Special Education*, 22(3): 100–4.

West, D. J. and Farrington, D. (1973) *Who becomes Delinquent?* London: Heinemann.

Westergaard, J. (1992) About and beyond the 'underclass': some notes on influences of social climate on British sociology today, *Sociology*, 26(4): 575–87.

Wolfendale, S. (ed.) (1989) *Parental Involvement: Developing Networks between School, Home and Community*. London: Cassell Educational.

York, R., Heron, J. M. and Wolff, S. (1972) Exclusion from school, *Journal of Child Psychology and Psychiatry*, 13: 259–66.

Young, M. and Halsey, A. H. (1995) *Family and Community Socialism*. IPPR Monograph. London: Institute for Public Policy Research.

Index

DISABILITY AND THE DILEMMAS OF EDUCATION AND JUSTICE

Carol Christensen and Fazal Rizvi (eds)

Debates about the education of people with disabilities are fundamentally moral and political, linked to concerns of justice. Compassion, care and equality have been central themes. Yet the field of special education is largely devoid of any explicit treatment of the ways in which educational justice might be understood. The essays in this book address issues of educational justice as they relate to people with disabilities. They suggest the need to move beyond deficit conceptions of difference and equality of access, articulated in the language of service delivery based on professional care and compassion, to a politics of recognition embedded within a framework of rights and empowerment.

Against this understanding of educational justice, it is argued that recent reforms in special education, which have promoted awareness of 'special needs', have not produced the changes envisaged by many reformers. The contributors to this book examine some of the current debates that resulted from the disillusionment of many teachers, researchers, policymakers and activists alike. They explore competing understandings of social justice in education; issues concerning the representation of disability and its articulation with gender, class and race; policies and practices of integration and inclusion; and dilemmas of professionalism in education.

The book is not located within a single disciplinary base. Rather, it draws upon a variety of disciplines, including philosophy, sociology, psychology and history in order to analyse issues concerning the relationship between disability, social justice and education. Equally it is international in scope, bringing together authors who have had a longstanding interest in issues of ethics, policy and practices of special education. It will be of interest and value to educationalists, social workers, researchers and policymakers.

Contents
Introduction – Disability, education and the discourses of justice – Disability and the education of persons – Educational ethics, social justice and children with disabilities – Disabled, handicapped or disordered – Disability, participation, representation and social justice – Disability, class and poverty – Coming out as gendered adults – 'The ideology of expertism' – Equity requires inclusion – Reforming special education – Conflicts and dilemmas for professionals in special education – Index.

Contributors
Carol Christensen, Alan Gartner, Michael M. Gerber, Kenneth R. Howe, Peter Isaacs, Andrew Jakubowicz, Bob Lingard, Dorothy Kerzner Lipsky, Genée Marks, Helen Meekosha, Fazal Rizvi, Roger Slee, Sally Tomlinson, Barry Troyna, Carol Vincent.

208pp   0 335 19583 0   (Paperback)   0 335 19584 9   (Hardback)

SPECIAL EDUCATIONAL NEEDS IN THE PRIMARY SCHOOL
(Second Edition)
A PRACTICAL GUIDE

Jean Gross

Reviews of the First Edition

'extraordinarily rich in ideas . . . an essential buy'

Times Educational Supplement

' . . . an excellent, clearly written work which is full of practical advice, and presented in an easily readable manner. This book is a highly recommended, ridiculously inexpensive read. Do buy it and see.'

Support for Learning

Recent legislation and cutbacks in central support services mean that the responsibility for meeting special educational needs is resting ever more squarely on the shoulders of ordinary classroom teachers. Yet few feel wholly confident in their ability to adapt work within the National Curriculum to meet the whole range of needs, or coordinate successful individual education plans for children who, for whatever reason, are not learning as well as they might.

This book will increase that confidence. Aimed at busy class teachers, special needs coordinators, heads and teachers in training, it shows how the teacher can build differentiation into planning lessons and schemes of work. It describes workable strategies for managing the most common behaviour difficulties and meeting special needs in language and mathematics.

At a whole school level, it offers practical guidance on developing special needs policies, assessment, record keeping, and the management of time, roles and resources. The focus is on the ways in which schools can do a good job in meeting special needs themselves, within everyday constraints of time, money and energy, and in doing so hold back the tide of increasing marginalization of vulnerable children within the education system.

Contents
Current perspectives on special educational needs – Developing a whole school policy – Special needs and the national curriculum – Assessment and special educational needs – Action planning and record keeping – Managing time – Managing roles and resources – Managing behaviour – Communication and classroom relationships – Special needs in speaking and listening – Special needs in reading – Special needs in writing – Special needs in maths – Beyond the school – References – Author index – Subject index.

272pp   0 335 19656 X   (Paperback)

BULLIES AND VICTIMS IN SCHOOLS
A GUIDE TO UNDERSTANDING AND MANAGEMENT

Valerie Besag

Bullying is a covert problem, buried in the subculture of a school. Even the most violent and consistent bullying can remain undetected, sometimes for years, until the victim finally cracks. The effects on victims can be pervasive and long term.

Valerie Besag examines what kind of child becomes a bully or victim, and why. She explores the family and social contexts which produce bullies and victims, and analyses the roles of race and gender.

She provides not only a guide to understanding bullying but also a teacher's handbook on what to do about it. She analyses how schools can provide an environment which *prevents* the occurrence of bullying; which protects against it but which can also respond effectively to crisis. She emphasizes the necessity for close home-school cooperation with parents and teachers as partners in helping both bully and victim.

This is an important and practical book in a neglected field which gives the basis for both understanding and action.

Contents
Introduction – Part 1: How to understand bullying – Researching bullying – The bullies – The victims – Family factors – Social behaviour – Part 2: What to do about bullying: a practical guide and checklist for teachers – The role of the school – Prevention – Protection – Parents as partners – Case studies – Appendix: workshop and curriculum material – Bibliography – Index.

232pp   0 335 09542 9 (Paperback)   0 335 09543 7 (Hardback)